THE GREAT EXPLORER OF MAMMOTH CAVE

A GRAPHIC NOVEL BIOGRAPHY OF
STEPHEN BISHOP

WRITTEN BY SHAWN PRYOR   ILLUSTRATED BY ALESSANDRO VALDRIGHI

CAPSTONE PRESS
a capstone imprint

Published by Capstone Press, an imprint of Capstone
1710 Roe Crest Drive, North Mankato, Minnesota 56003
capstonepub.com

Library of Congress Cataloging-in-Publication Data
Names: Pryor, Shawn, author. | Valdrighi, Alessandro, illustrator.
Title: The great explorer of Mammoth Cave : a graphic novel biography of
Stephen Bishop / by Shawn Pryor ; illustrated by Alessandro Valdrighi.
Description: North Mankato, Minnesota : Capstone Press, [2024] | Series:
Barrier breakers | Includes bibliographical references. | Audience: Ages 8-11
| Audience: Grades 4-6 | Summary: "Mammoth Cave, a National Park near
Brownsville, Kentucky, is the world's largest cavern with more than 400 miles of
cavern space. The first to explore the cave was an enslaved Black man, Stephen
Bishop. With bravery and a curious mind, Bishop became a popular tour guide
and mapped out the extensive caverns, all while remaining enslaved. Learn about
this respected explorer's work in this inspiring graphic novel"— Provided by
publisher.
Identifiers: LCCN 2023019150 (print) | LCCN 2023019151 (ebook) |
ISBN 9781669061762 (hardcover) | ISBN 9781669061946 (paperback) |
ISBN 9781669061809 (pdf) | ISBN 9781669061960 (kindle edition) |
ISBN 9781669061953 (epub)
Subjects: LCSH: Bishop, Stephen, 1821?-1857—Comic books, strips, etc.—Juvenile
literature. | African American explorers—Biography—Juvenile literature. |
African American explorers—Biography—Comic books, strips, etc. | Enslaved
persons—Kentucky—Mammoth Cave—Biography—Juvenile literature. |
Enslaved persons—Kentucky—Mammoth Cave—Biography—Comic books,
strips, etc. | Spelunkers—United States—Biography—Juvenile literature. |
Spelunkers—United States—Biography—Comic books, strips, etc. | Caving—
Kentucky—Mammoth Cave—Juvenile literature. | Caving—Kentucky—
Mammoth Cave—Comic books, strips, etc. | Graphic novels—Juvenile
literature. | Mammoth Cave (Ky.)—History—Juvenile literature. | Kentucky—
History—1792-1865—Juvenile literature.
Classification: LCC G226.B57 P78 2024 (print) | LCC G226.B57 (ebook) |
DDC 976.9/754092—dc23/eng/20230525
LC record available at https://lccn.loc.gov/2023019150
LC ebook record available at https://lccn.loc.gov/2023019151

Editorial Credits
Editor: Julie Gassman; Designer: Dina Her; Production Specialist: Tori Abraham

Image Credit
Library of Congress, 28

Printed and bound in the USA. 5626

TABLE OF CONTENTS

The Mammoth Cave and Stephen Bishop

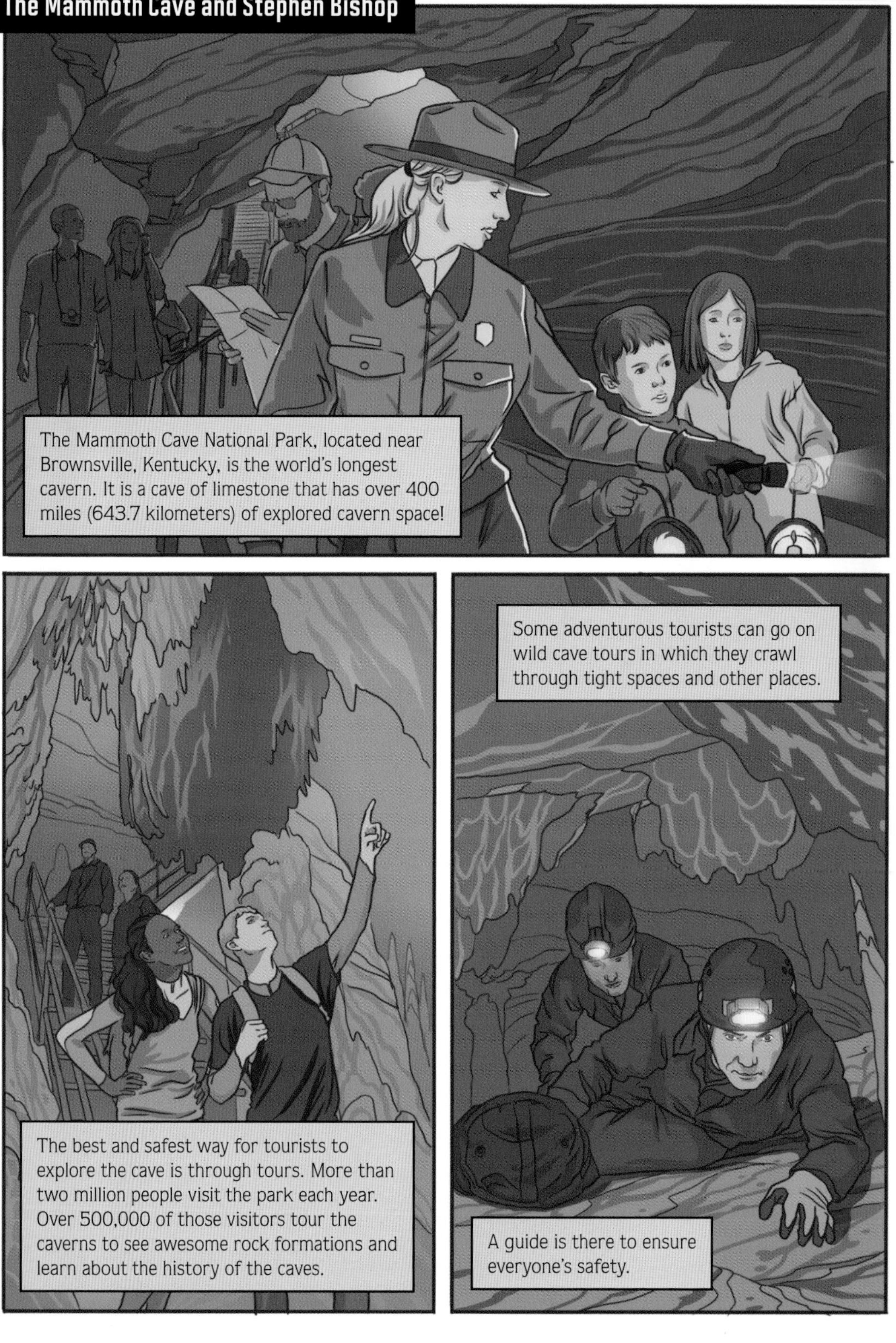
The Mammoth Cave National Park, located near Brownsville, Kentucky, is the world's longest cavern. It is a cave of limestone that has over 400 miles (643.7 kilometers) of explored cavern space!
The best and safest way for tourists to explore the cave is through tours. More than two million people visit the park each year. Over 500,000 of those visitors tour the caverns to see awesome rock formations and learn about the history of the caves.
Some adventurous tourists can go on wild cave tours in which they crawl through tight spaces and other places.
A guide is there to ensure everyone's safety.

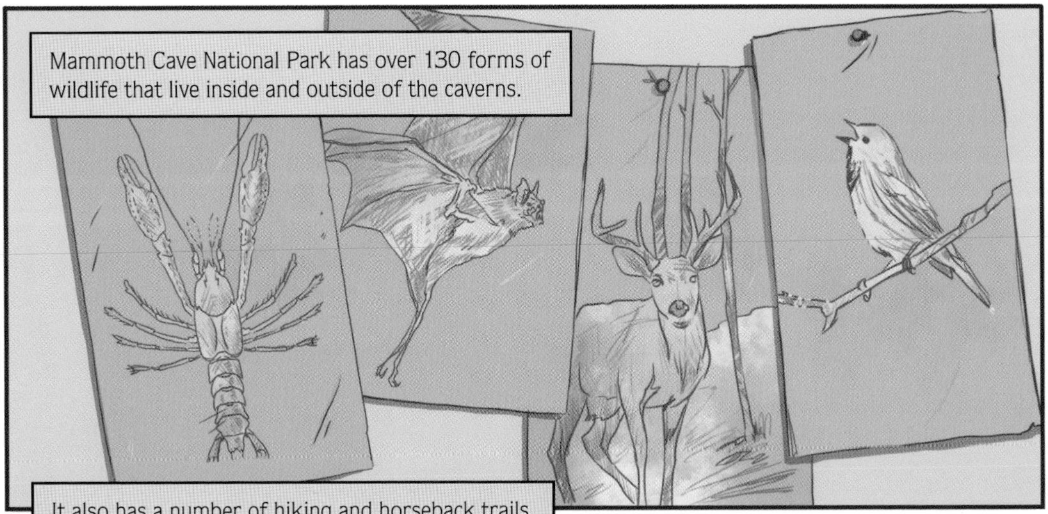
Mammoth Cave National Park has over 130 forms of wildlife that live inside and outside of the caverns.

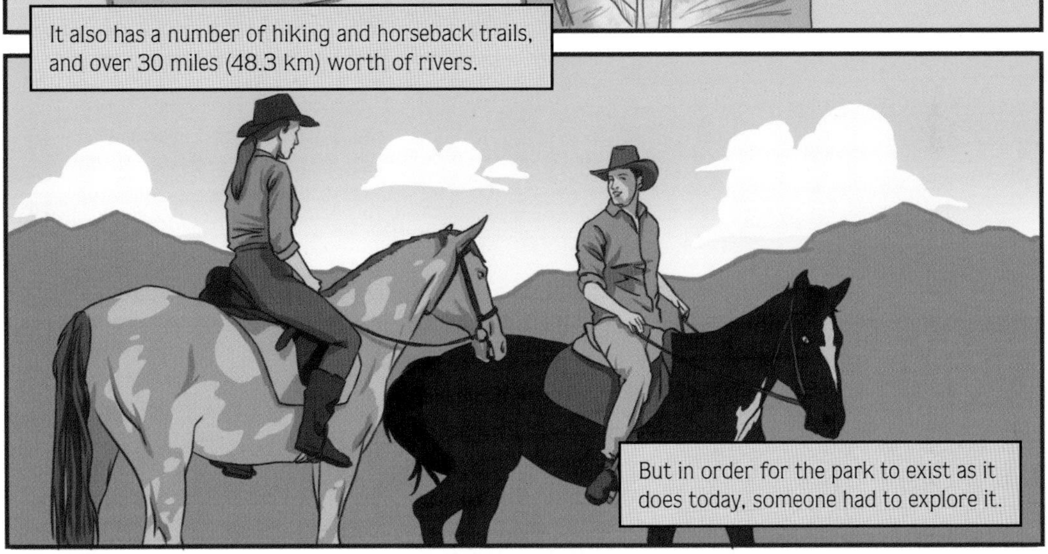
It also has a number of hiking and horseback trails, and over 30 miles (48.3 km) worth of rivers.
But in order for the park to exist as it does today, someone had to explore it.

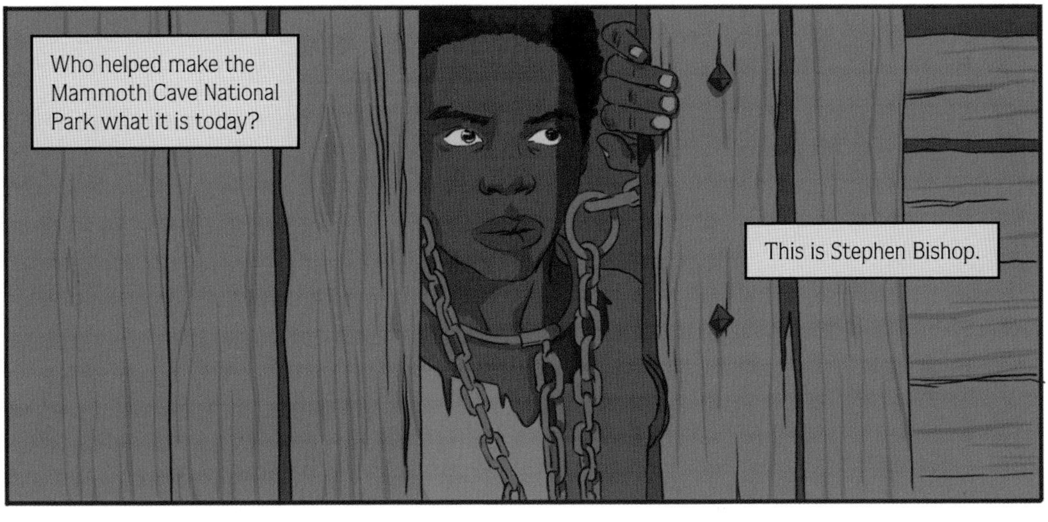
Who helped make the Mammoth Cave National Park what it is today?
This is Stephen Bishop.

An Explorer's Start

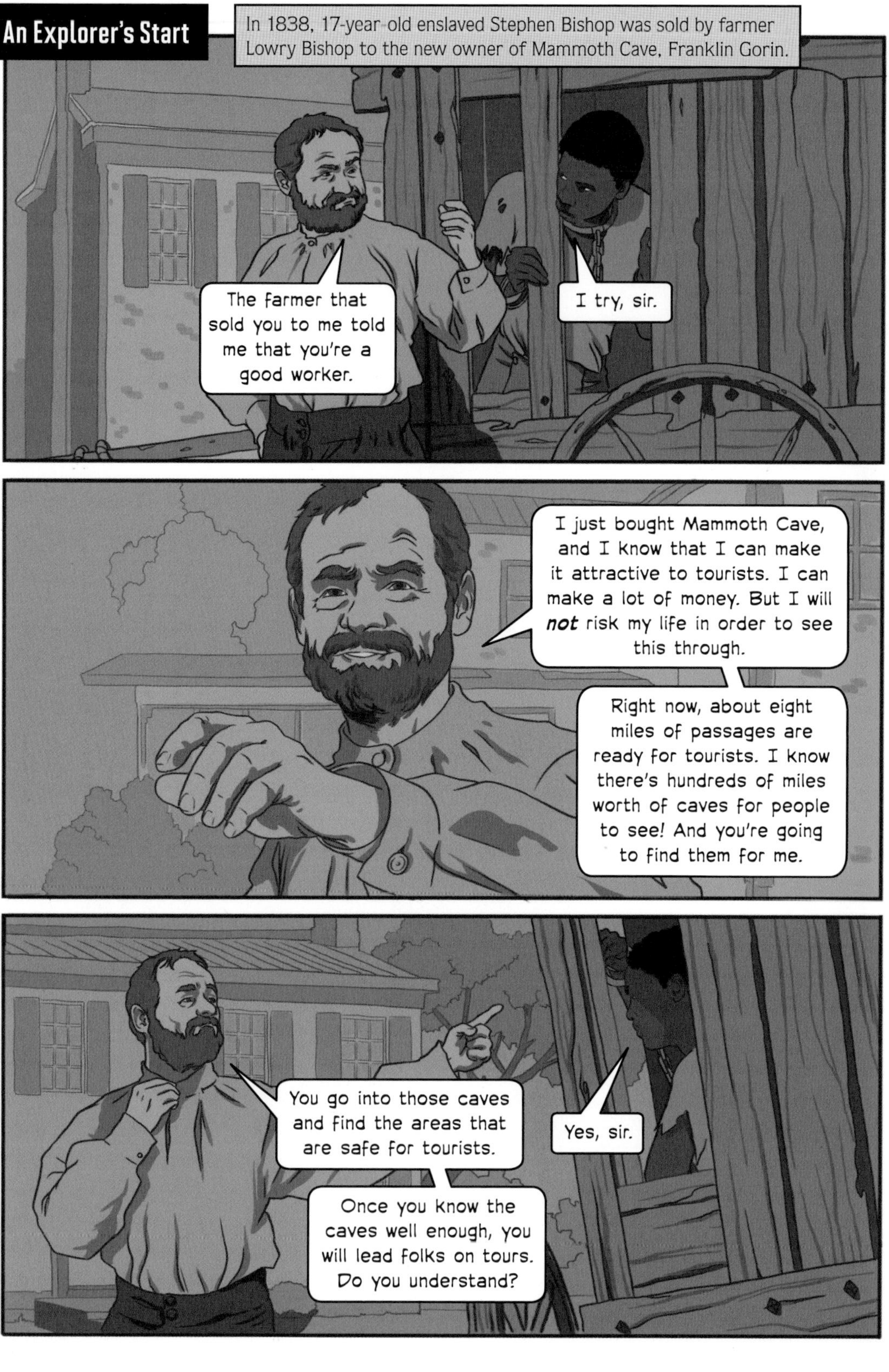

In 1838, 17-year-old enslaved Stephen Bishop was sold by farmer Lowry Bishop to the new owner of Mammoth Cave, Franklin Gorin.
The farmer that sold you to me told me that you're a good worker.
I try, sir.
I just bought Mammoth Cave, and I know that I can make it attractive to tourists. I can make a lot of money. But I will *not* risk my life in order to see this through.
Right now, about eight miles of passages are ready for tourists. I know there's hundreds of miles worth of caves for people to see! And you're going to find them for me.
You go into those caves and find the areas that are safe for tourists.
Once you know the caves well enough, you will lead folks on tours. Do you understand?
Yes, sir.

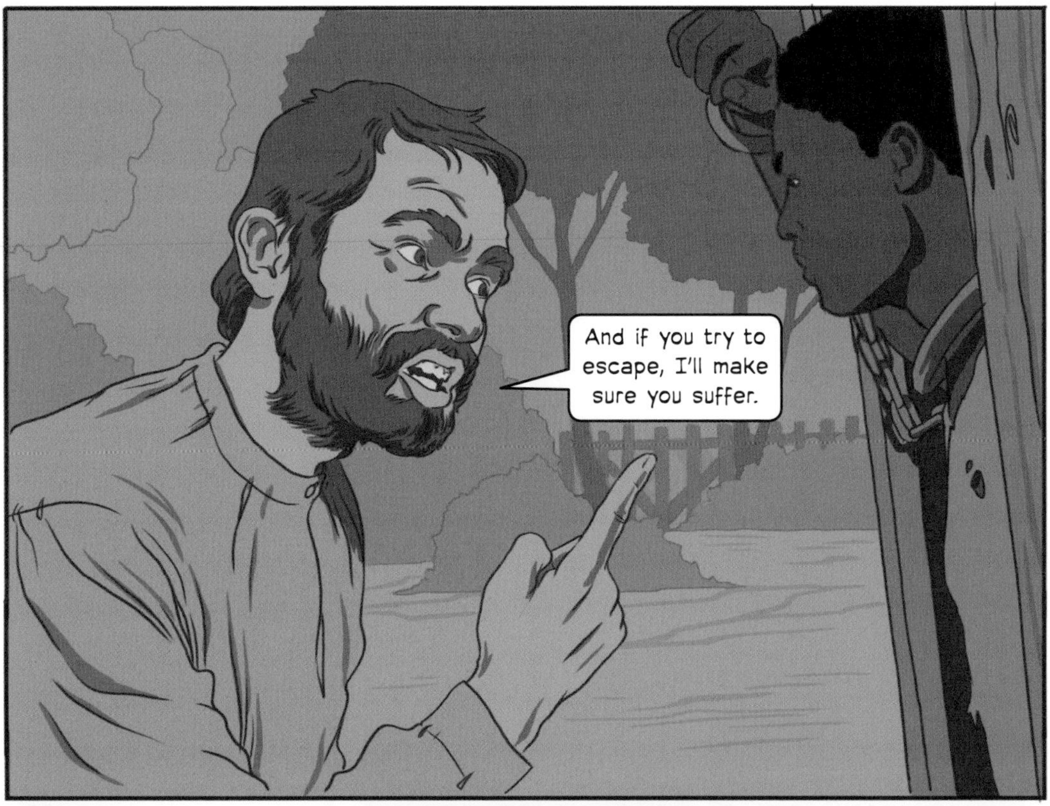
And if you try to escape, I'll make sure you suffer.

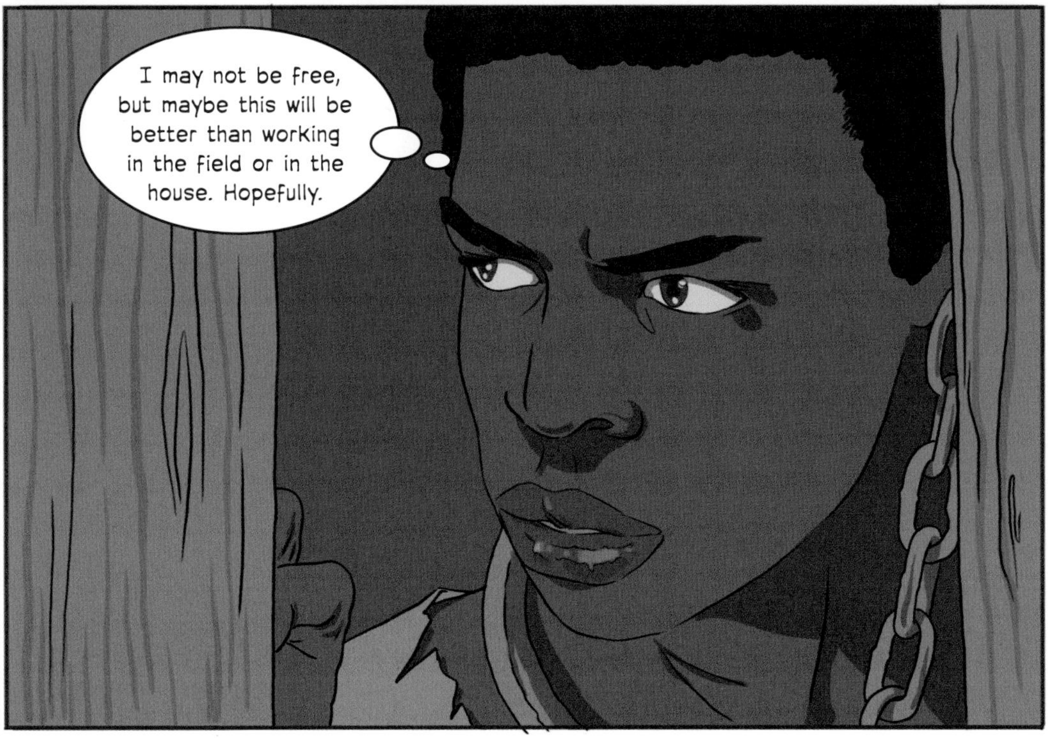
I may not be free, but maybe this will be better than working in the field or in the house. Hopefully.

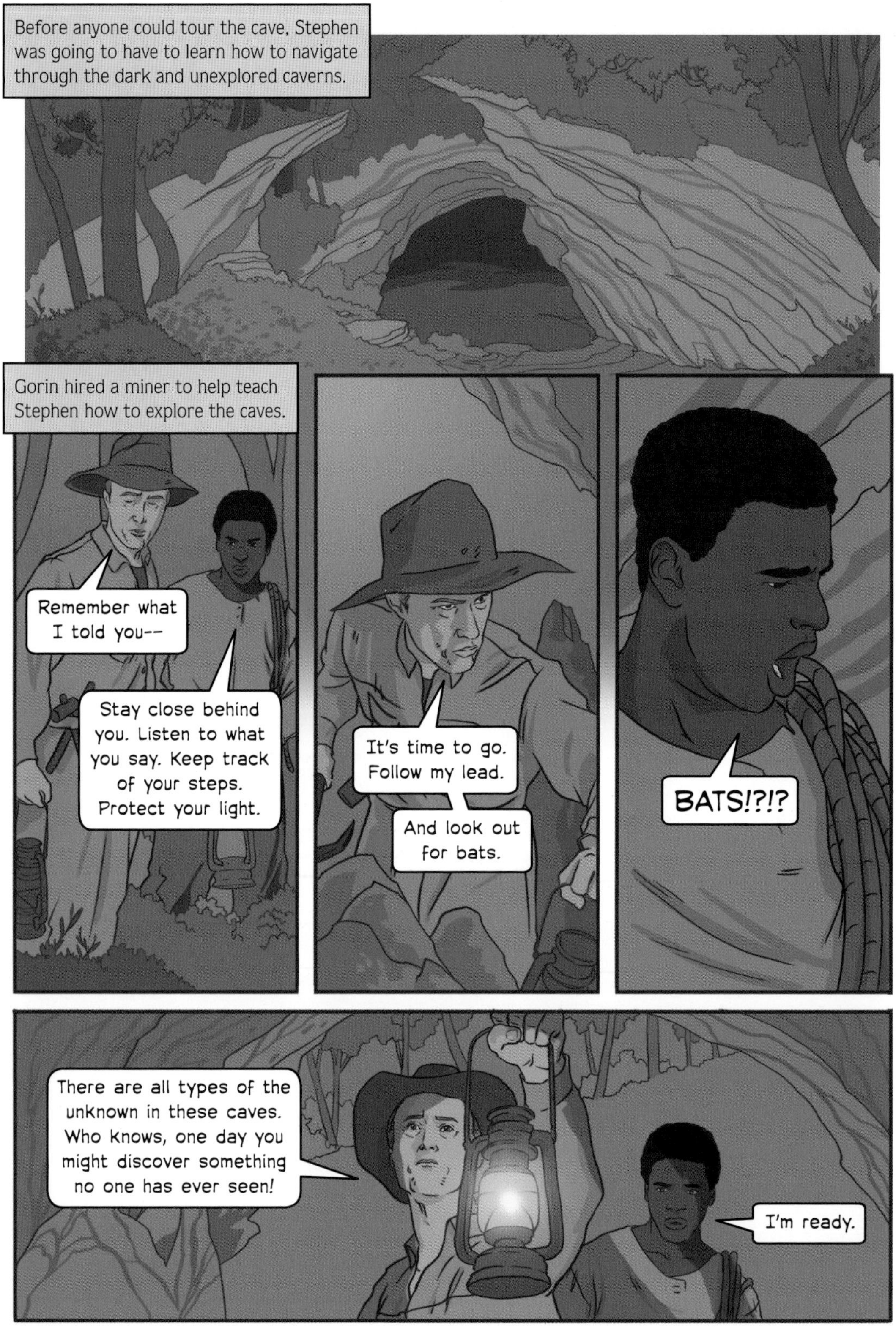
Before anyone could tour the cave, Stephen was going to have to learn how to navigate through the dark and unexplored caverns.
Gorin hired a miner to help teach Stephen how to explore the caves.
Remember what I told you--
Stay close behind you. Listen to what you say. Keep track of your steps. Protect your light.
It's time to go. Follow my lead.
And look out for bats.
BATS!?!?
There are all types of the unknown in these caves. Who knows, one day you might discover something no one has ever seen!
I'm ready.

Cavern Explorer

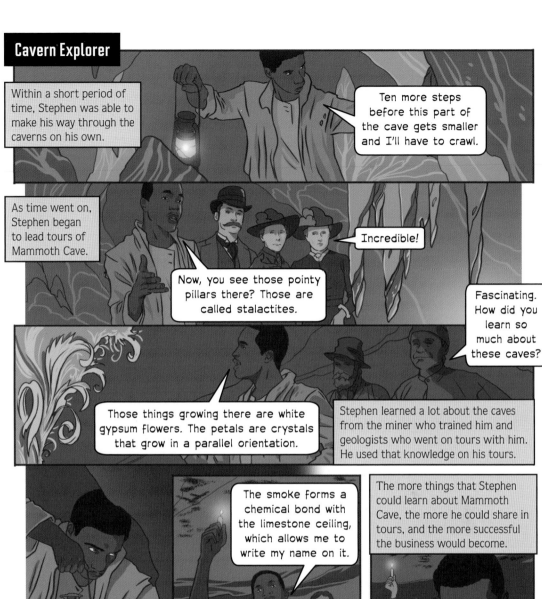

Within a short period of time, Stephen was able to make his way through the caverns on his own.

Ten more steps before this part of the cave gets smaller and I'll have to crawl.

As time went on, Stephen began to lead tours of Mammoth Cave.

Incredible!

Now, you see those pointy pillars there? Those are called stalactites.

Fascinating. How did you learn so much about these caves?

Those things growing there are white gypsum flowers. The petals are crystals that grow in a parallel orientation.

Stephen learned a lot about the caves from the miner who trained him and geologists who went on tours with him. He used that knowledge on his tours.

The smoke forms a chemical bond with the limestone ceiling, which allows me to write my name on it.

The more things that Stephen could learn about Mammoth Cave, the more he could share in tours, and the more successful the business would become.

And when he wasn't leading tours, his time was spent searching for new safe paths for tourists to travel.

WOW! Dad- Dad- give our guide some extra money so we can write our names on the ceiling!

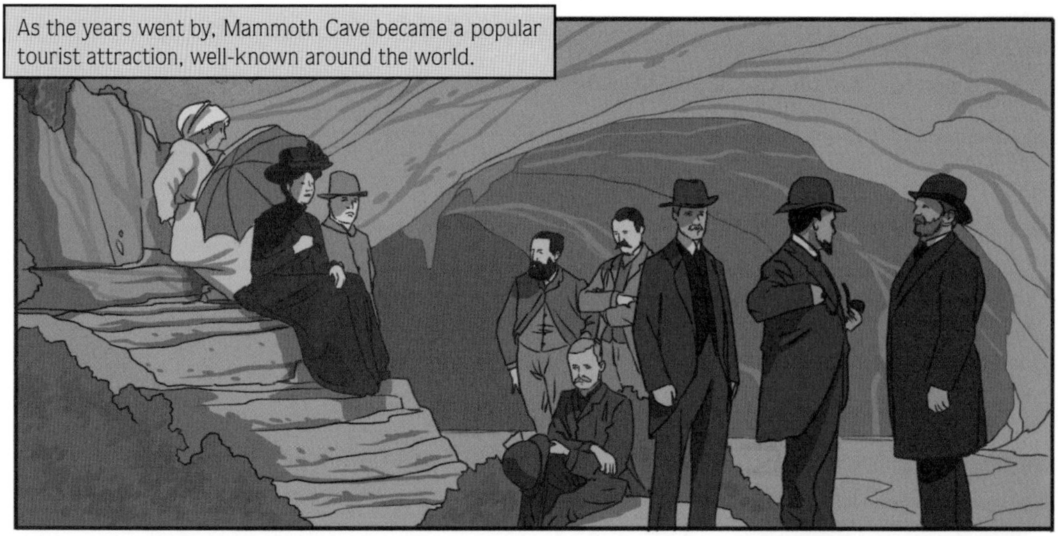
As the years went by, Mammoth Cave became a popular tourist attraction, well-known around the world.

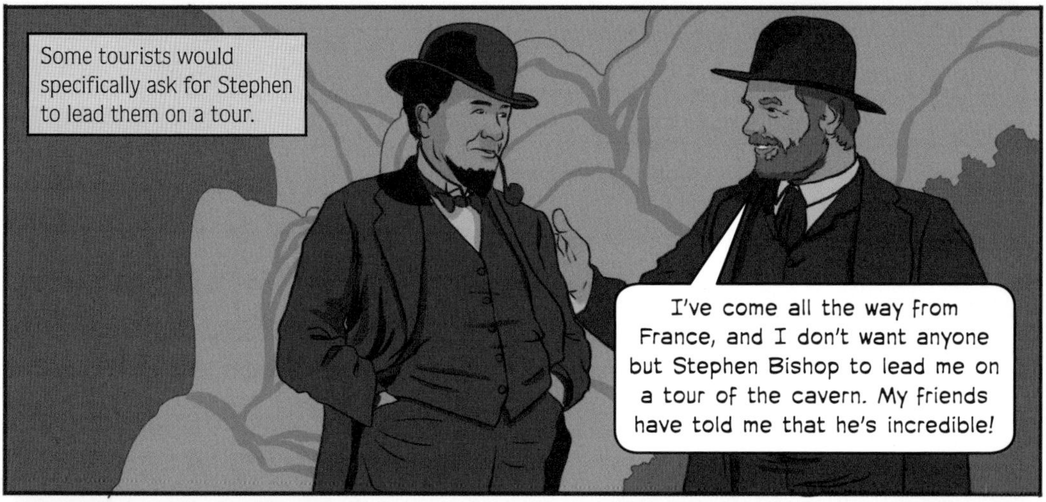
Some tourists would specifically ask for Stephen to lead them on a tour.
I've come all the way from France, and I don't want anyone but Stephen Bishop to lead me on a tour of the cavern. My friends have told me that he's incredible!

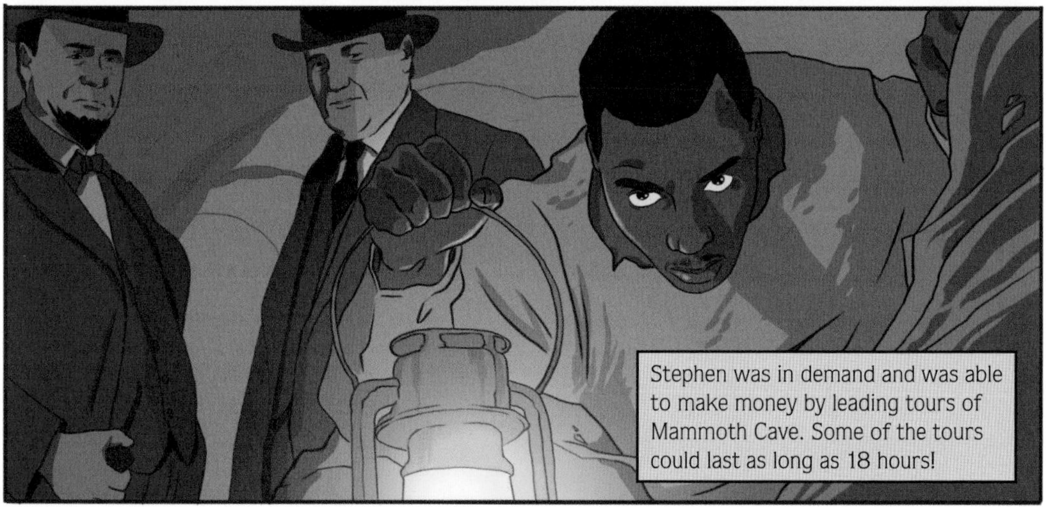
Stephen was in demand and was able to make money by leading tours of Mammoth Cave. Some of the tours could last as long as 18 hours!

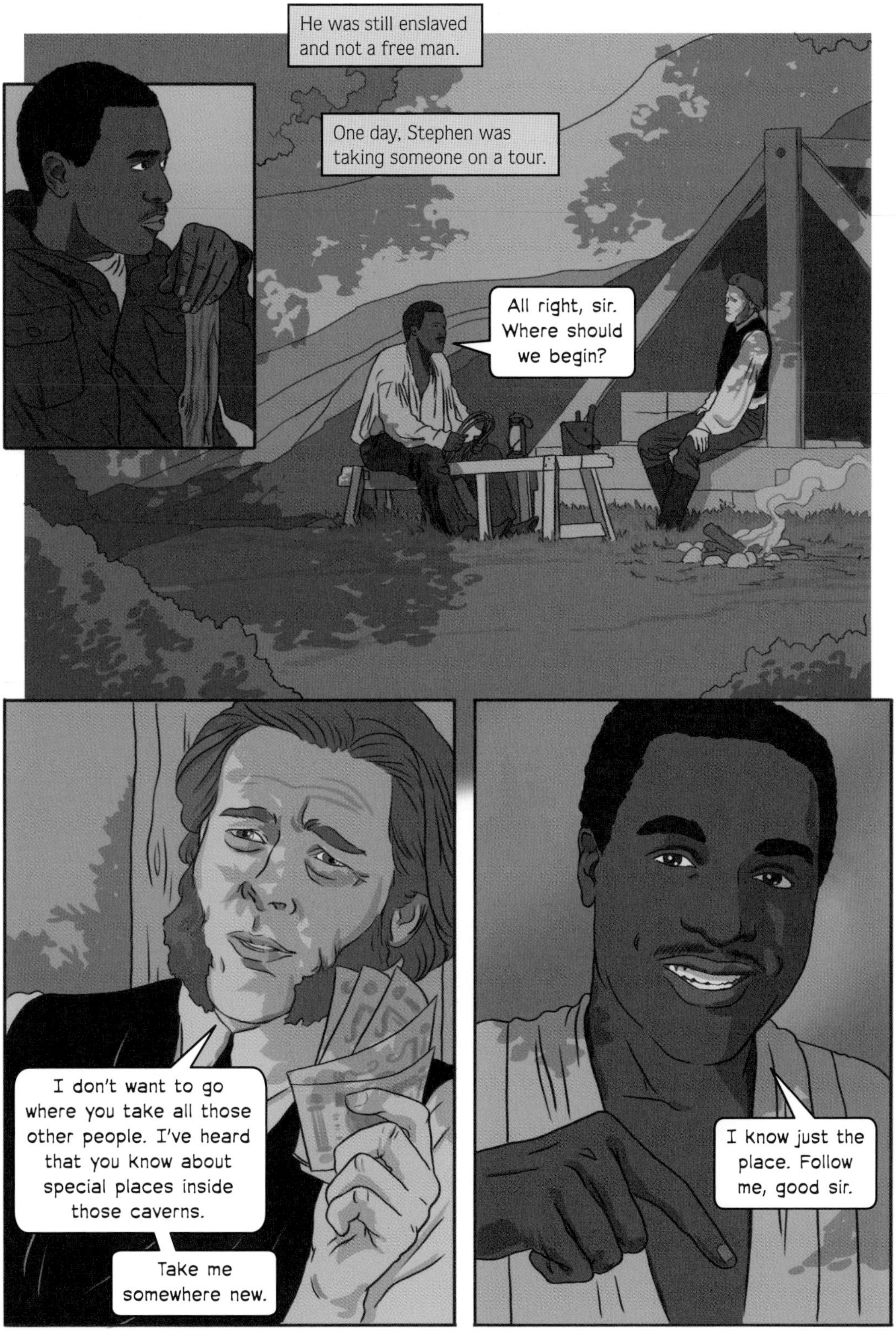
He was still enslaved and not a free man.
One day, Stephen was taking someone on a tour.
All right, sir. Where should we begin?
I don't want to go where you take all those other people. I've heard that you know about special places inside those caverns.
Take me somewhere new.
I know just the place. Follow me, good sir.

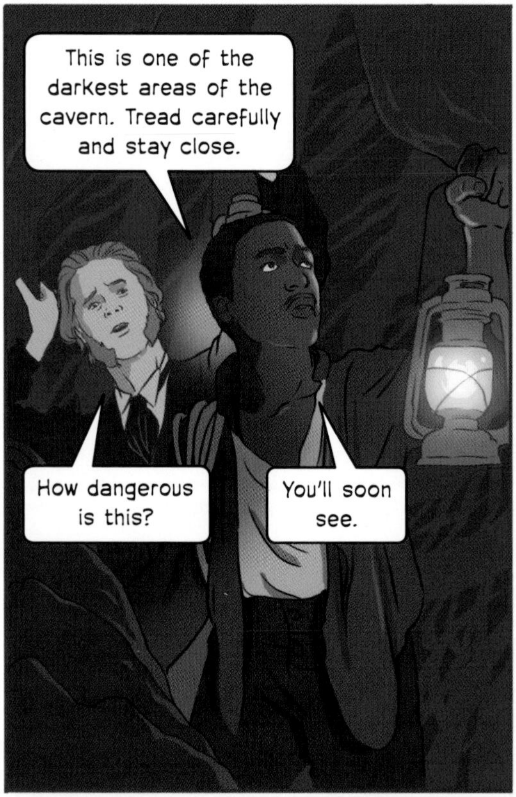
This is one of the darkest areas of the cavern. Tread carefully and stay close.
How dangerous is this?
You'll soon see.

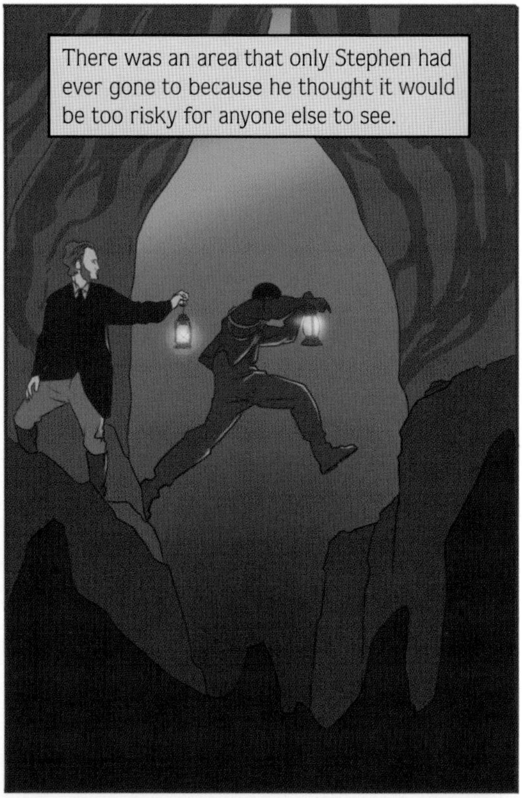
There was an area that only Stephen had ever gone to because he thought it would be too risky for anyone else to see.

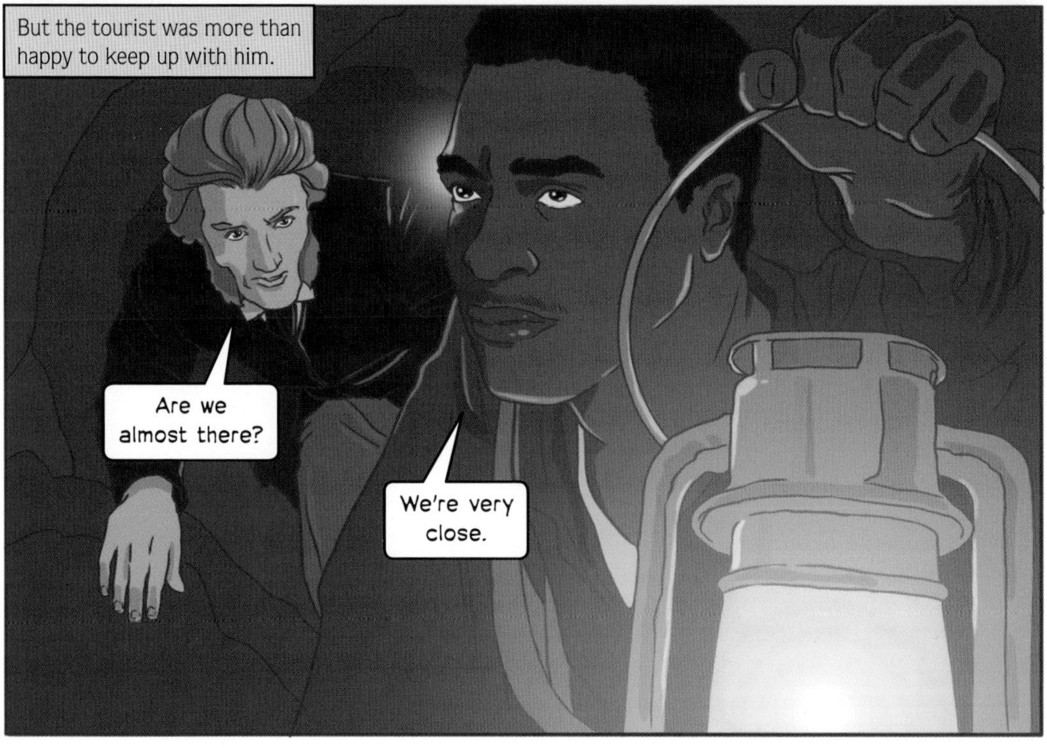
But the tourist was more than happy to keep up with him.
Are we almost there?
We're very close.

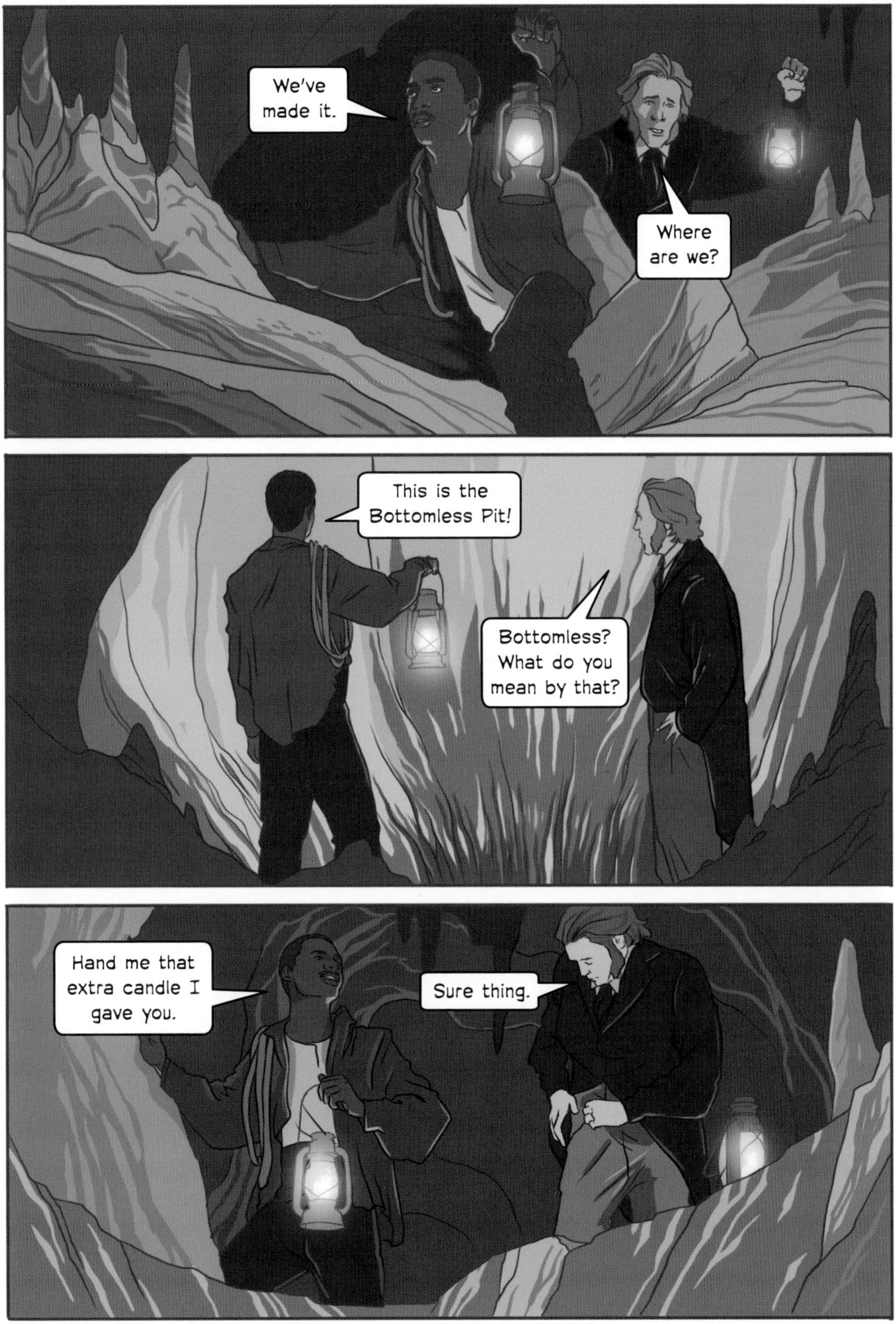

We've made it.
Where are we?
This is the Bottomless Pit!
Bottomless? What do you mean by that?
Hand me that extra candle I gave you.
Sure thing.

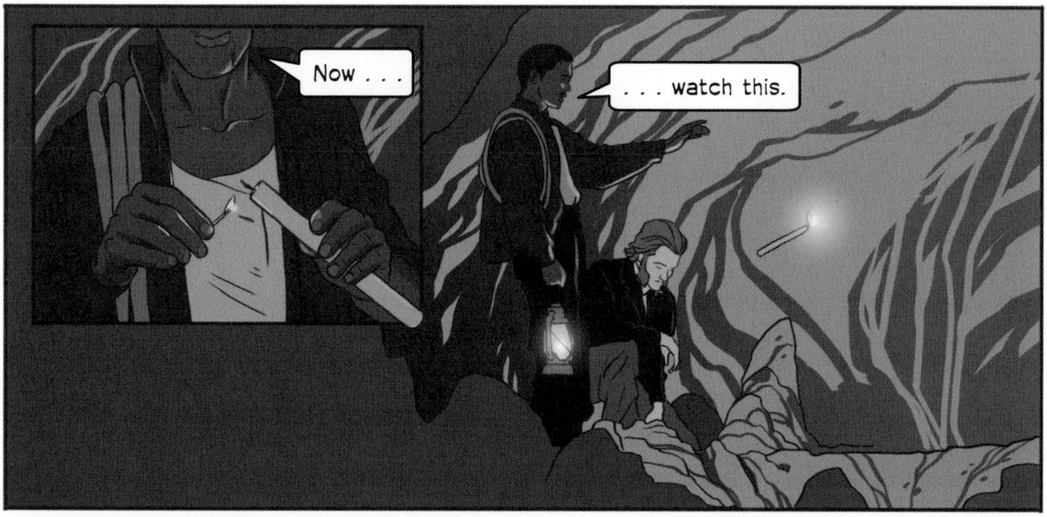
Now . . .
. . . watch this.

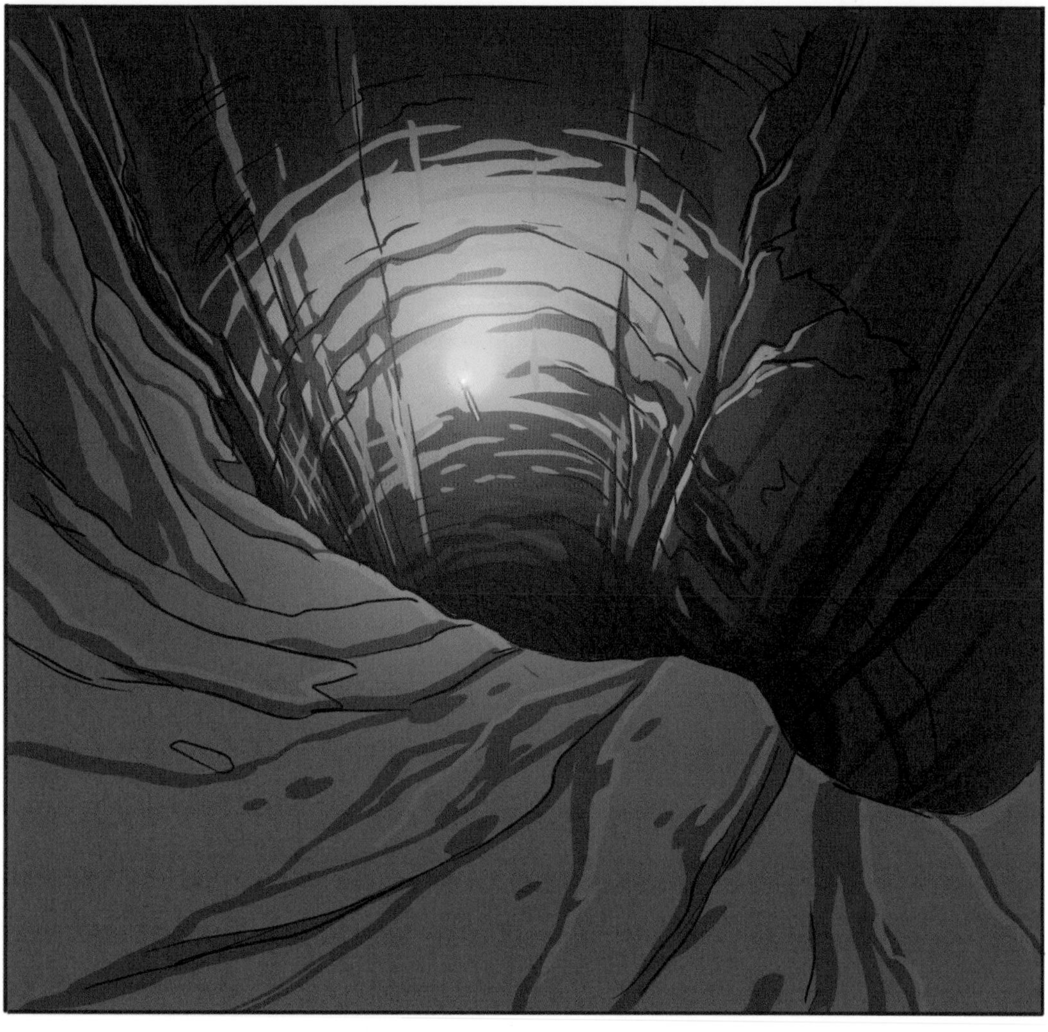

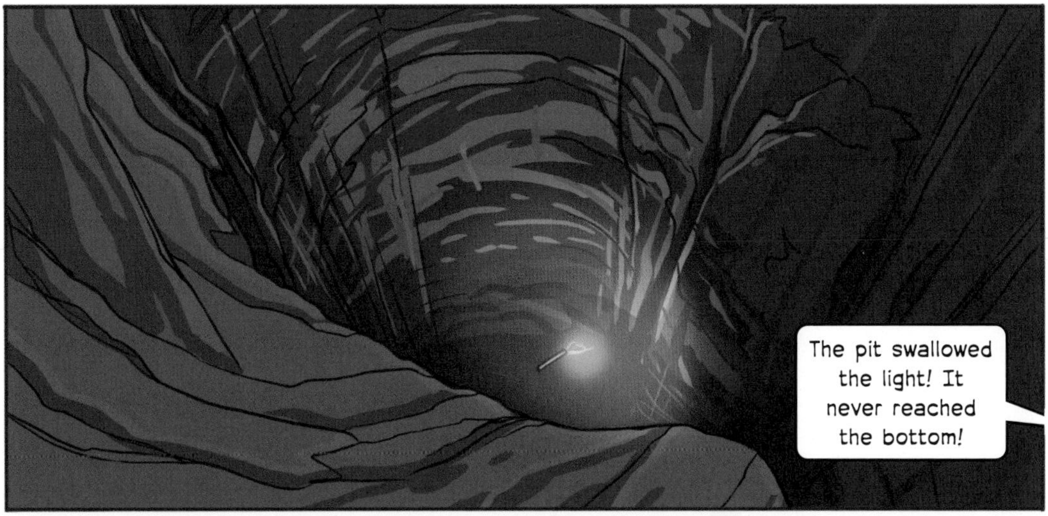
The pit swallowed the light! It never reached the bottom!

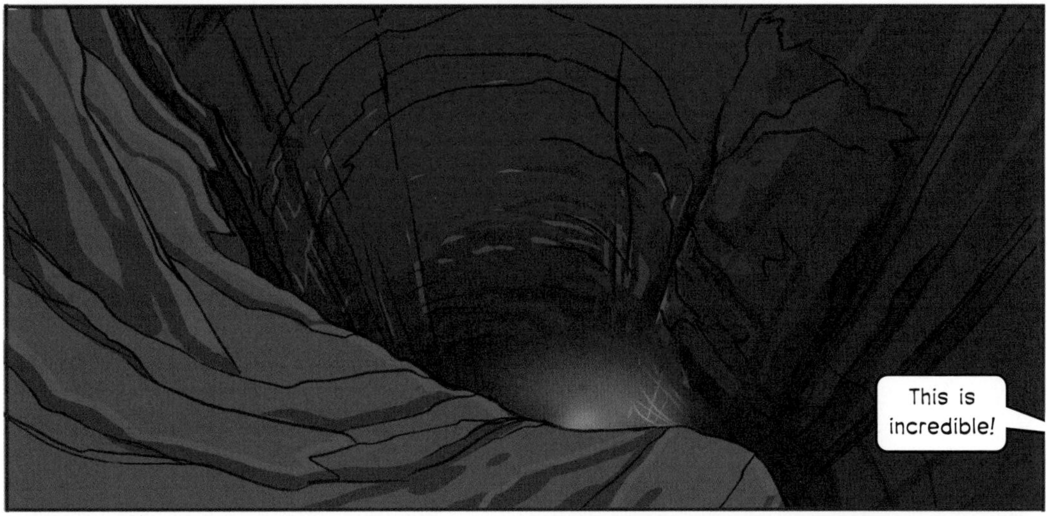
This is incredible!

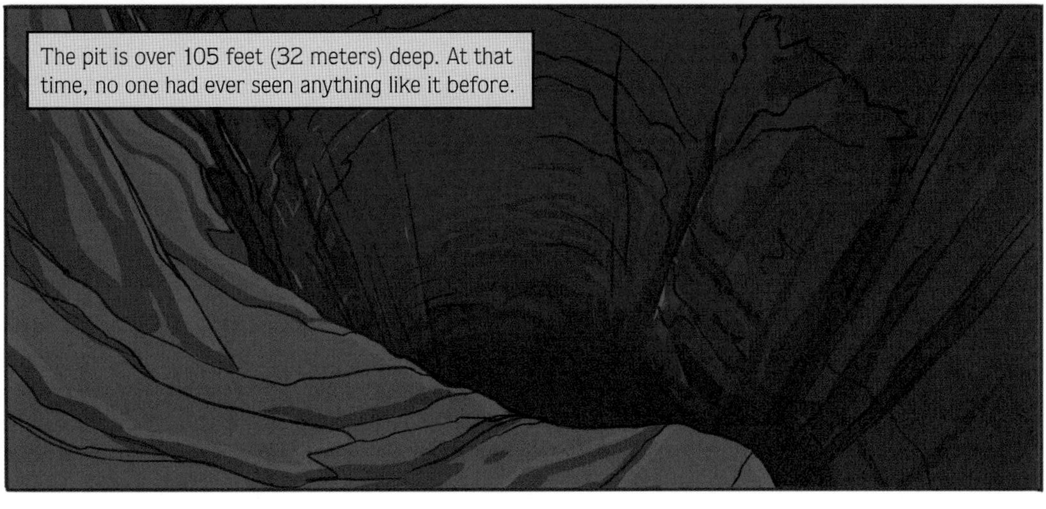
The pit is over 105 feet (32 meters) deep. At that time, no one had ever seen anything like it before.

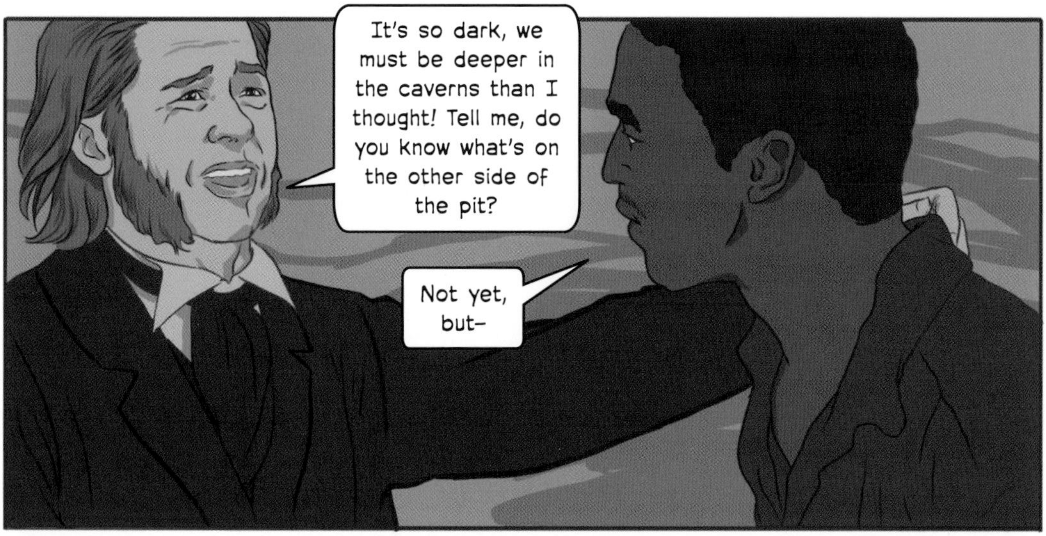
It's so dark, we must be deeper in the caverns than I thought! Tell me, do you know what's on the other side of the pit?
Not yet, but–

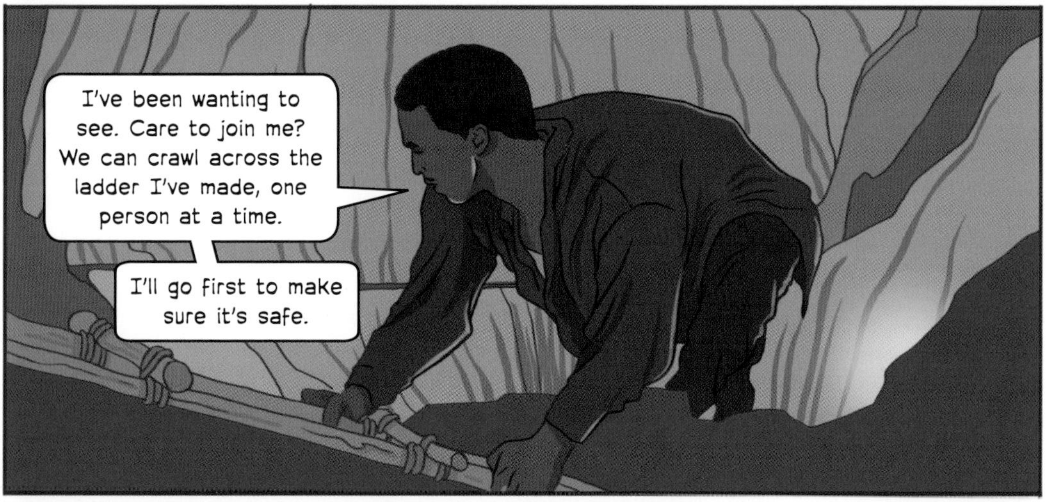
I've been wanting to see. Care to join me? We can crawl across the ladder I've made, one person at a time.
I'll go first to make sure it's safe.

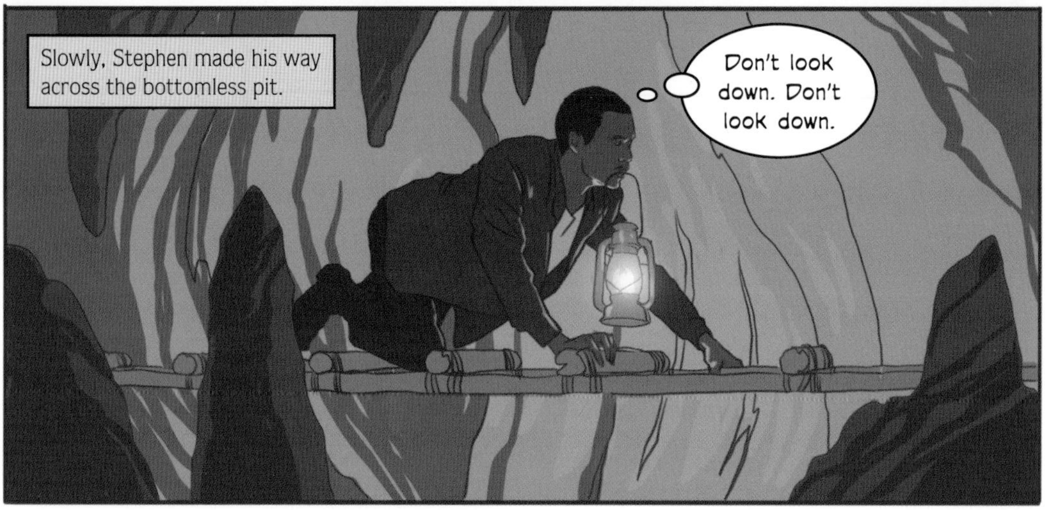
Slowly, Stephen made his way across the bottomless pit.
Don't look down. Don't look down.

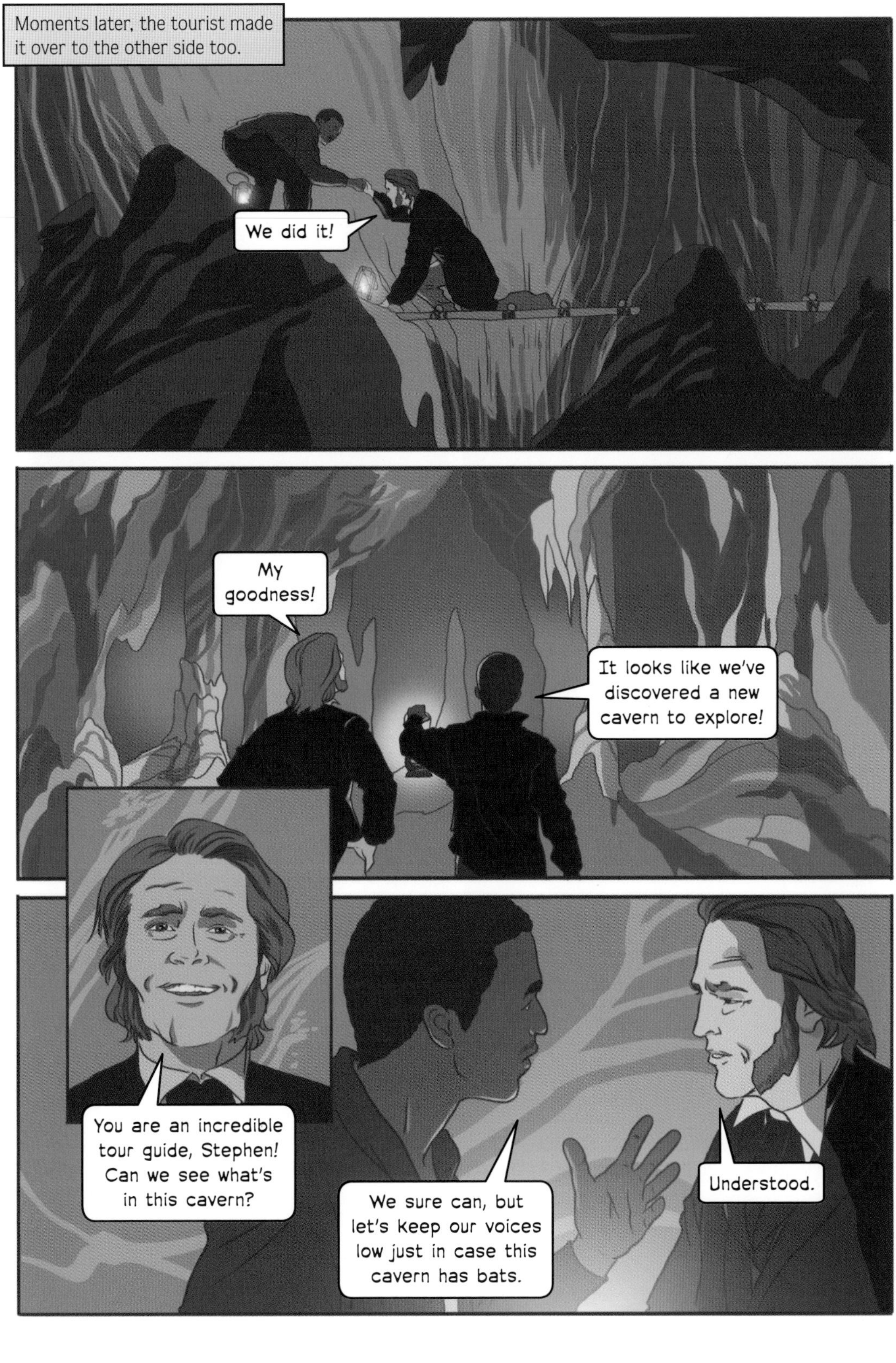
Moments later, the tourist made it over to the other side too.
We did it!
My goodness!
It looks like we've discovered a new cavern to explore!
You are an incredible tour guide, Stephen! Can we see what's in this cavern?
We sure can, but let's keep our voices low just in case this cavern has bats.
Understood.

Rivers and Maps

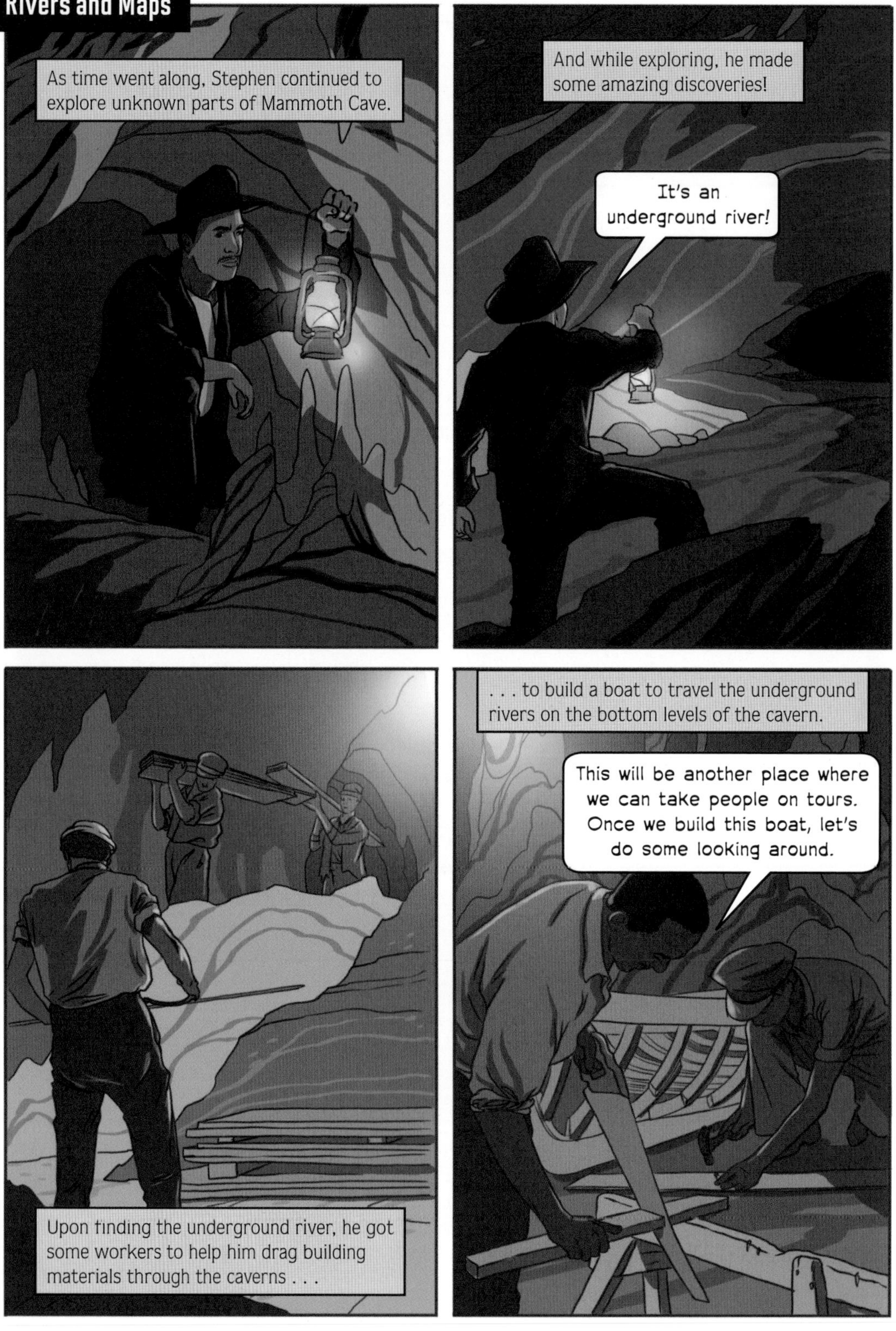

As time went along, Stephen continued to explore unknown parts of Mammoth Cave.
And while exploring, he made some amazing discoveries!
It's an underground river!
Upon finding the underground river, he got some workers to help him drag building materials through the caverns . . .
. . . to build a boat to travel the underground rivers on the bottom levels of the cavern.
This will be another place where we can take people on tours. Once we build this boat, let's do some looking around.

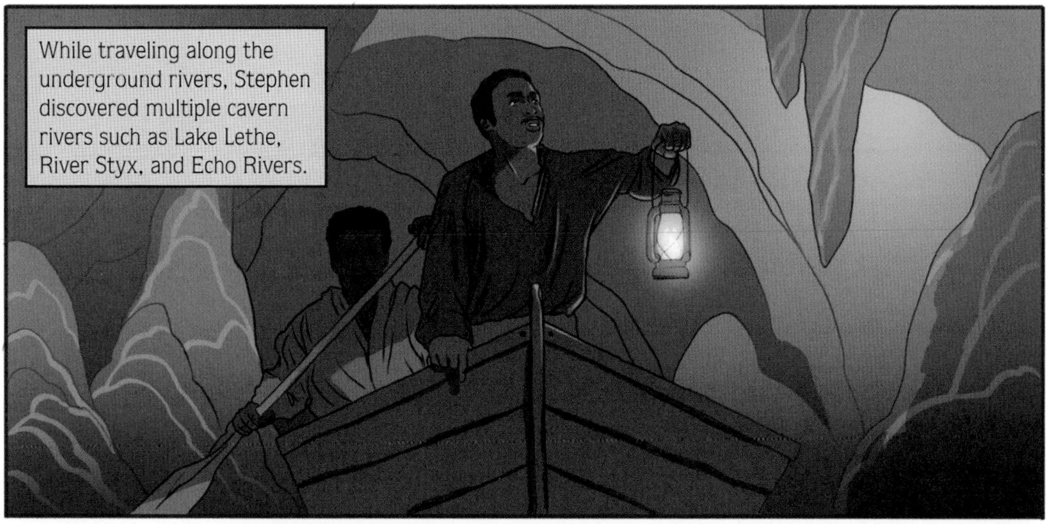
While traveling along the underground rivers, Stephen discovered multiple cavern rivers such as Lake Lethe, River Styx, and Echo Rivers.

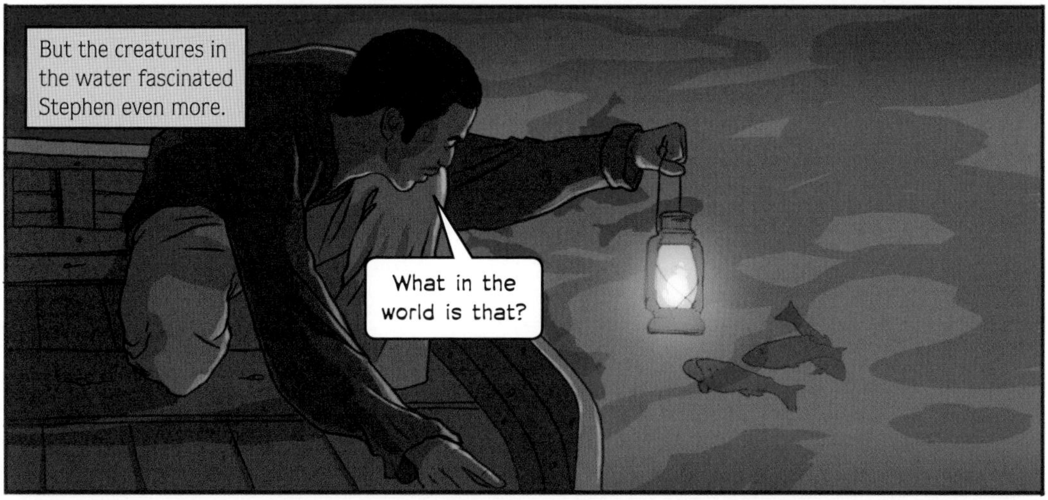
But the creatures in the water fascinated Stephen even more.
What in the world is that?

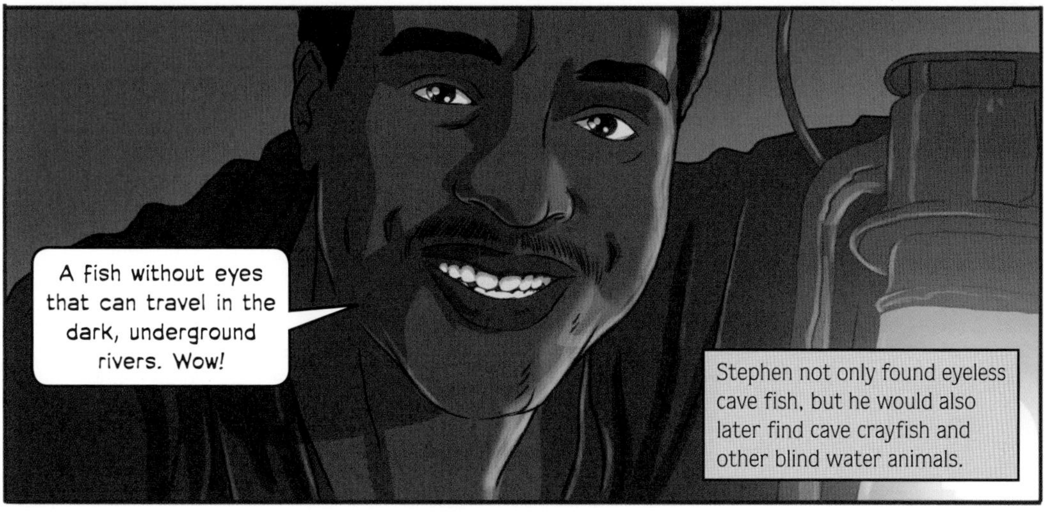
A fish without eyes that can travel in the dark, underground rivers. Wow!
Stephen not only found eyeless cave fish, but he would also later find cave crayfish and other blind water animals.

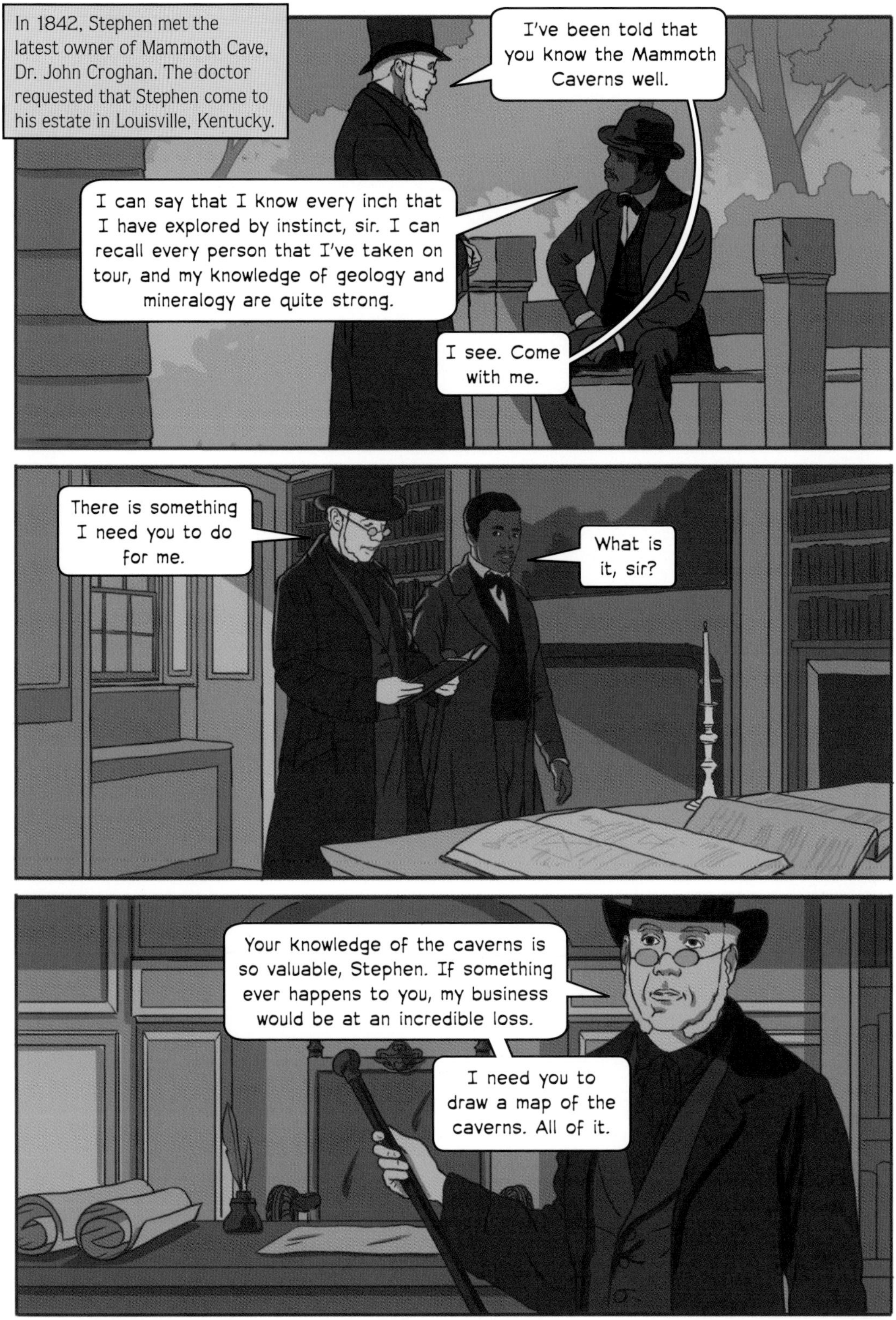
In 1842, Stephen met the latest owner of Mammoth Cave, Dr. John Croghan. The doctor requested that Stephen come to his estate in Louisville, Kentucky.
I've been told that you know the Mammoth Caverns well.
I can say that I know every inch that I have explored by instinct, sir. I can recall every person that I've taken on tour, and my knowledge of geology and mineralogy are quite strong.
I see. Come with me.
There is something I need you to do for me.
What is it, sir?
Your knowledge of the caverns is so valuable, Stephen. If something ever happens to you, my business would be at an incredible loss.
I need you to draw a map of the caverns. All of it.

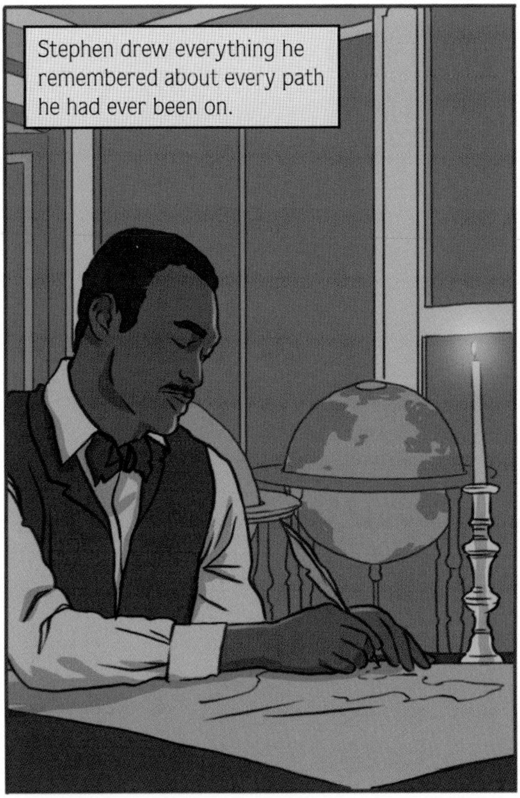
Stephen drew everything he remembered about every path he had ever been on.

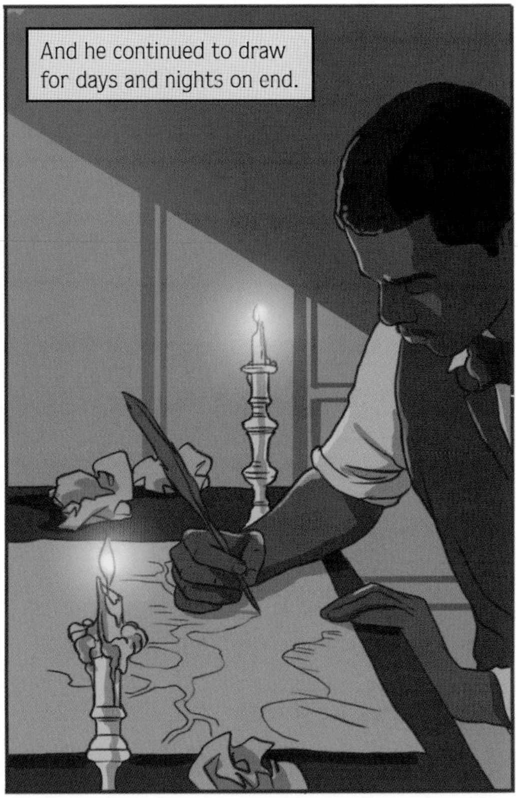
And he continued to draw for days and nights on end.

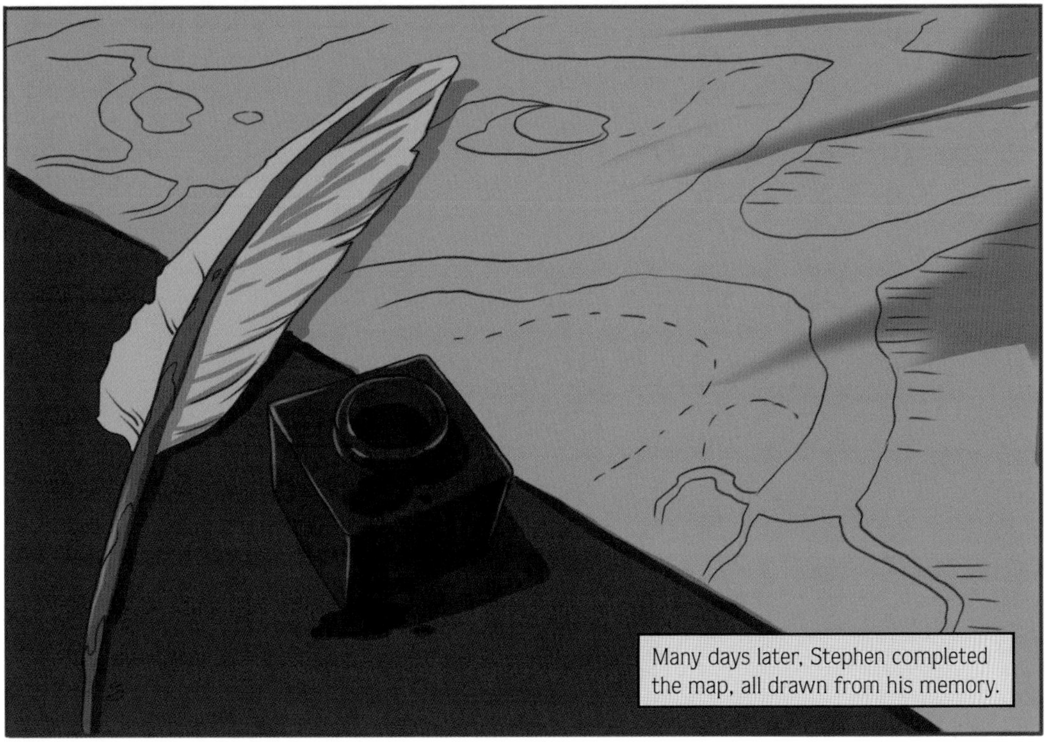
Many days later, Stephen completed the map, all drawn from his memory.

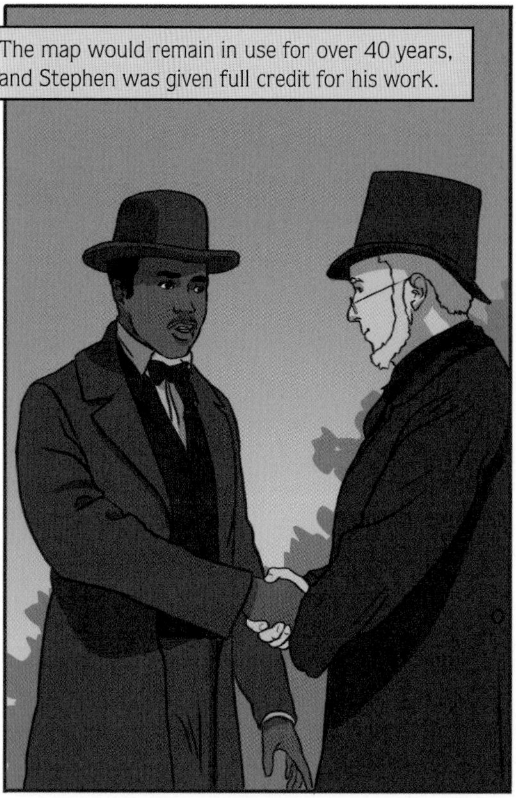
The map would remain in use for over 40 years, and Stephen was given full credit for his work.

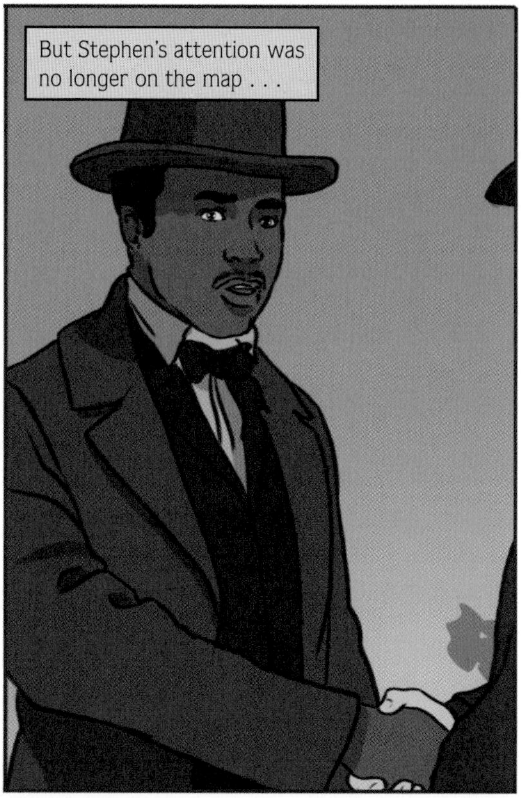
But Stephen's attention was no longer on the map . . .

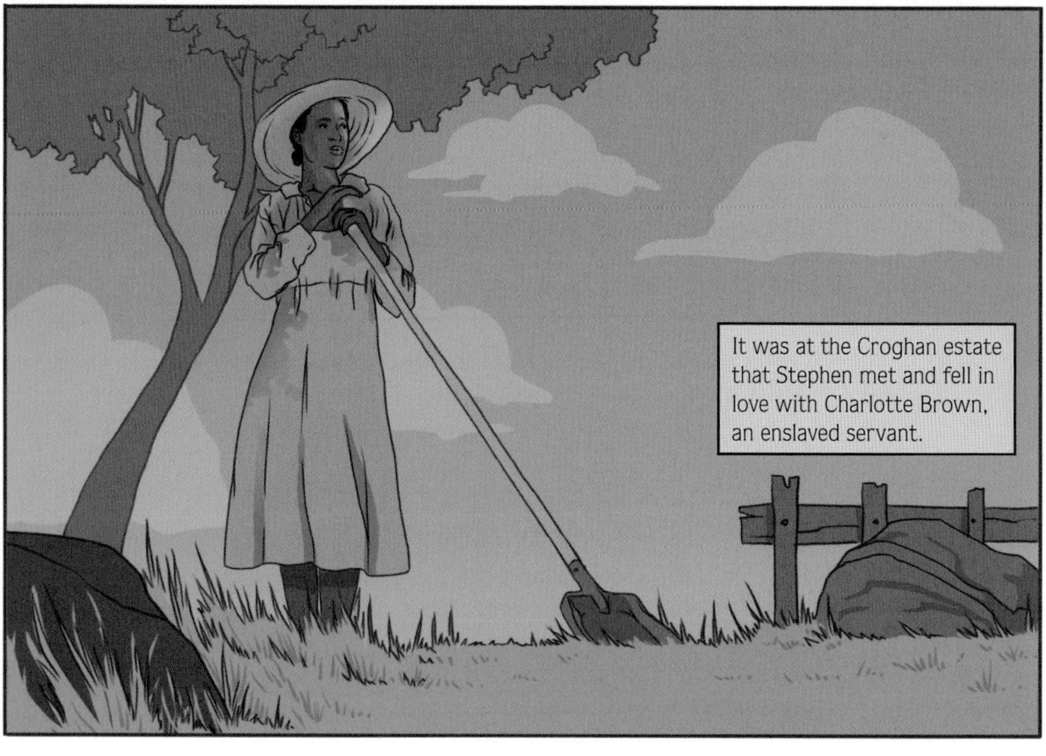
It was at the Croghan estate that Stephen met and fell in love with Charlotte Brown, an enslaved servant.

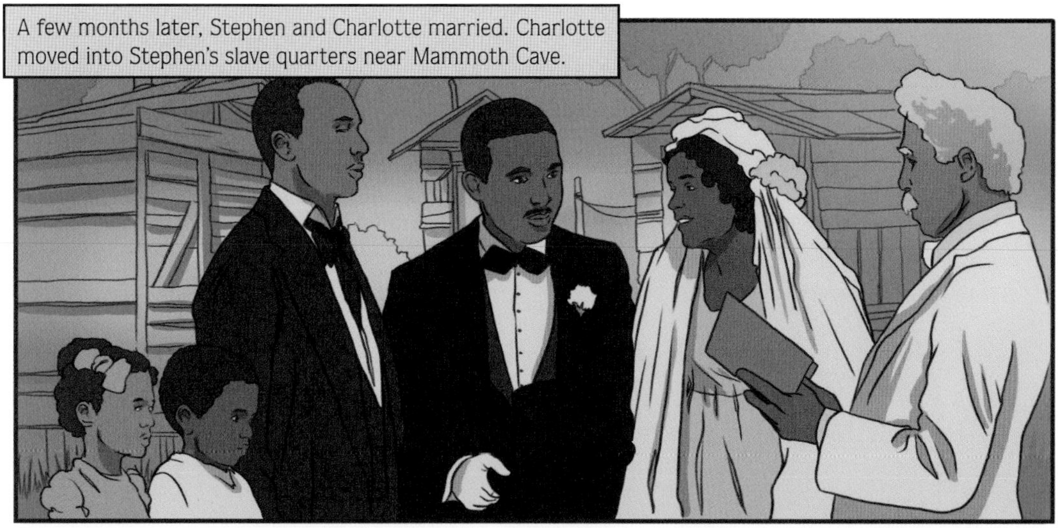
A few months later, Stephen and Charlotte married. Charlotte moved into Stephen's slave quarters near Mammoth Cave.

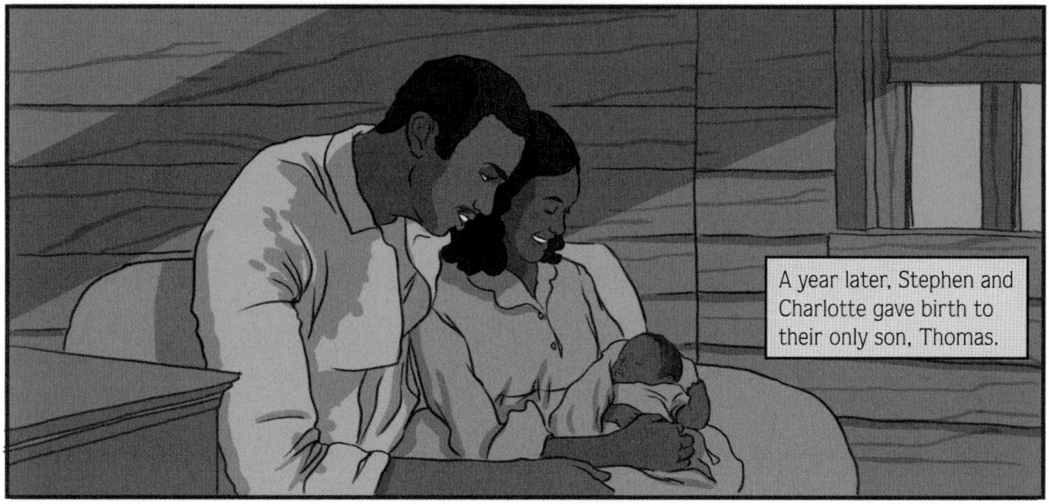
A year later, Stephen and Charlotte gave birth to their only son, Thomas.

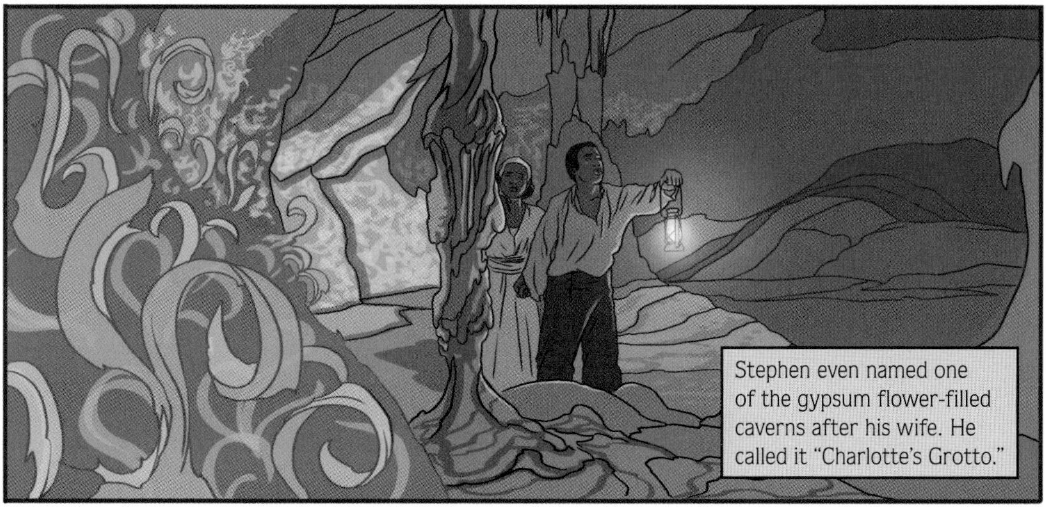
Stephen even named one of the gypsum flower-filled caverns after his wife. He called it "Charlotte's Grotto."

Finally Free

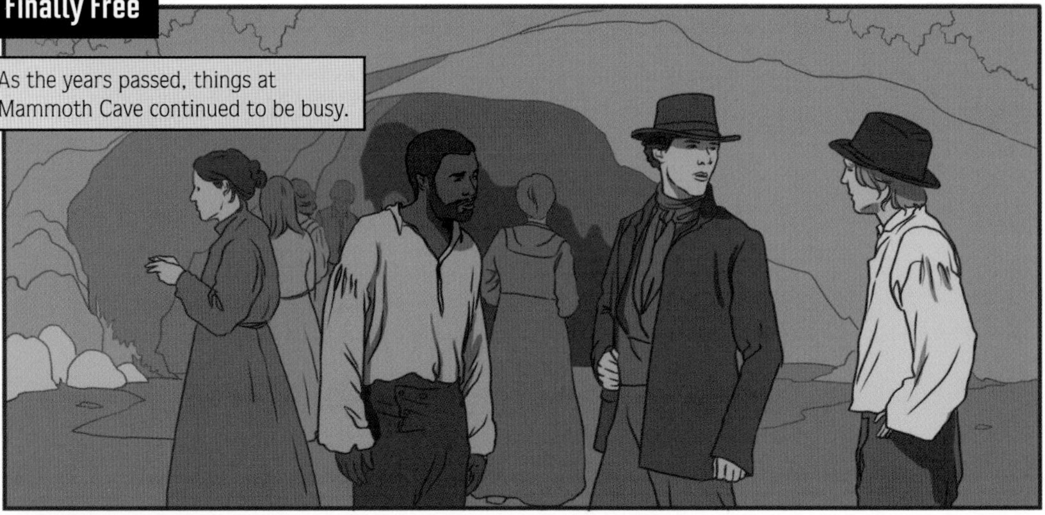
As the years passed, things at Mammoth Cave continued to be busy.

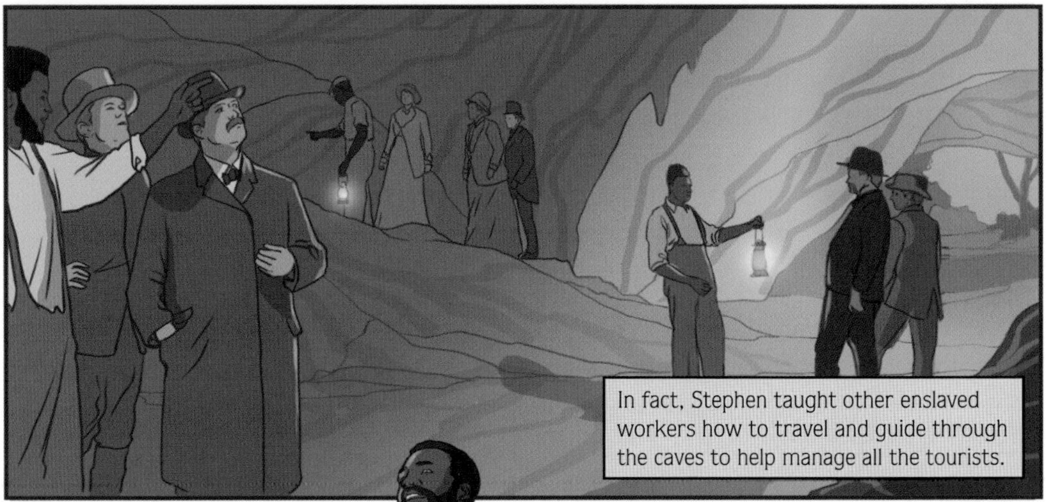
In fact, Stephen taught other enslaved workers how to travel and guide through the caves to help manage all the tourists.

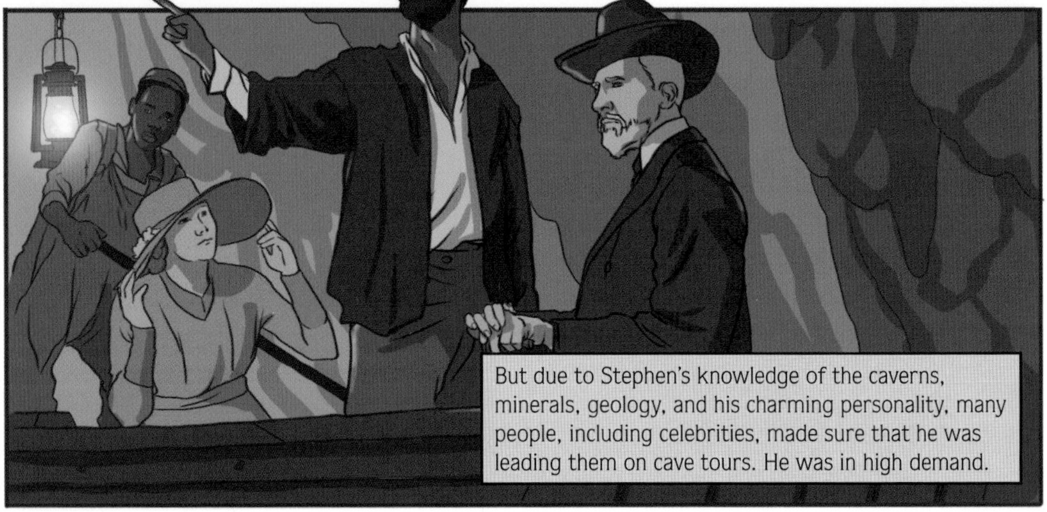
But due to Stephen's knowledge of the caverns, minerals, geology, and his charming personality, many people, including celebrities, made sure that he was leading them on cave tours. He was in high demand.

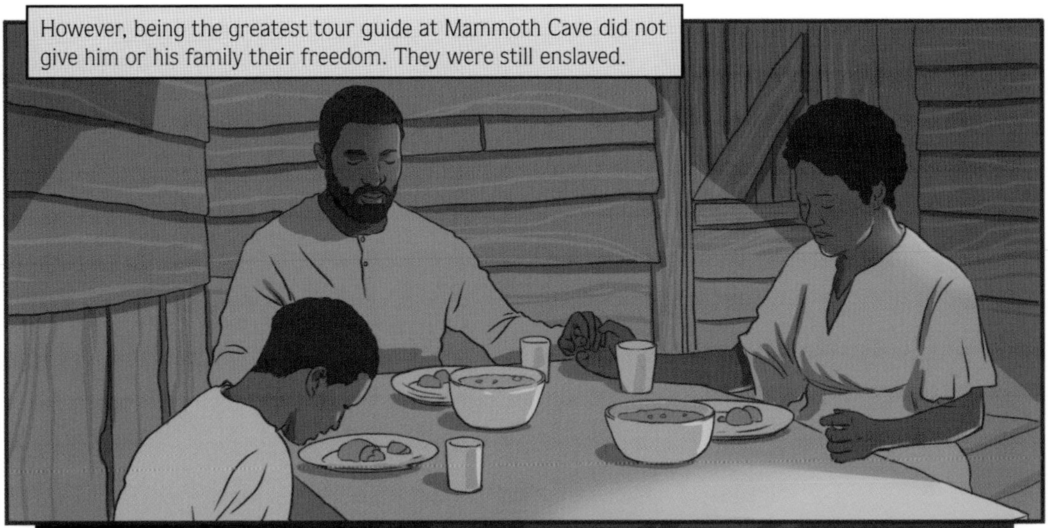
However, being the greatest tour guide at Mammoth Cave did not give him or his family their freedom. They were still enslaved.

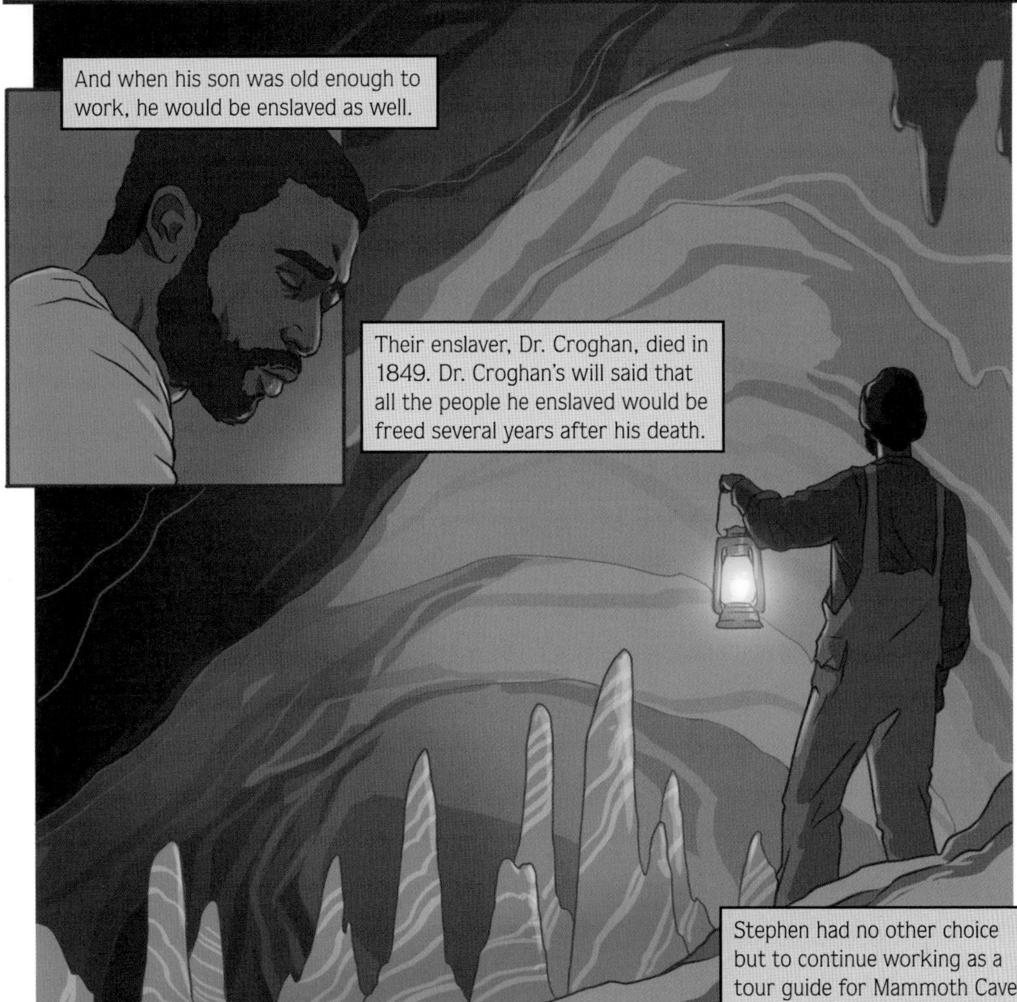
And when his son was old enough to work, he would be enslaved as well.
Their enslaver, Dr. Croghan, died in 1849. Dr. Croghan's will said that all the people he enslaved would be freed several years after his death.
Stephen had no other choice but to continue working as a tour guide for Mammoth Cave.

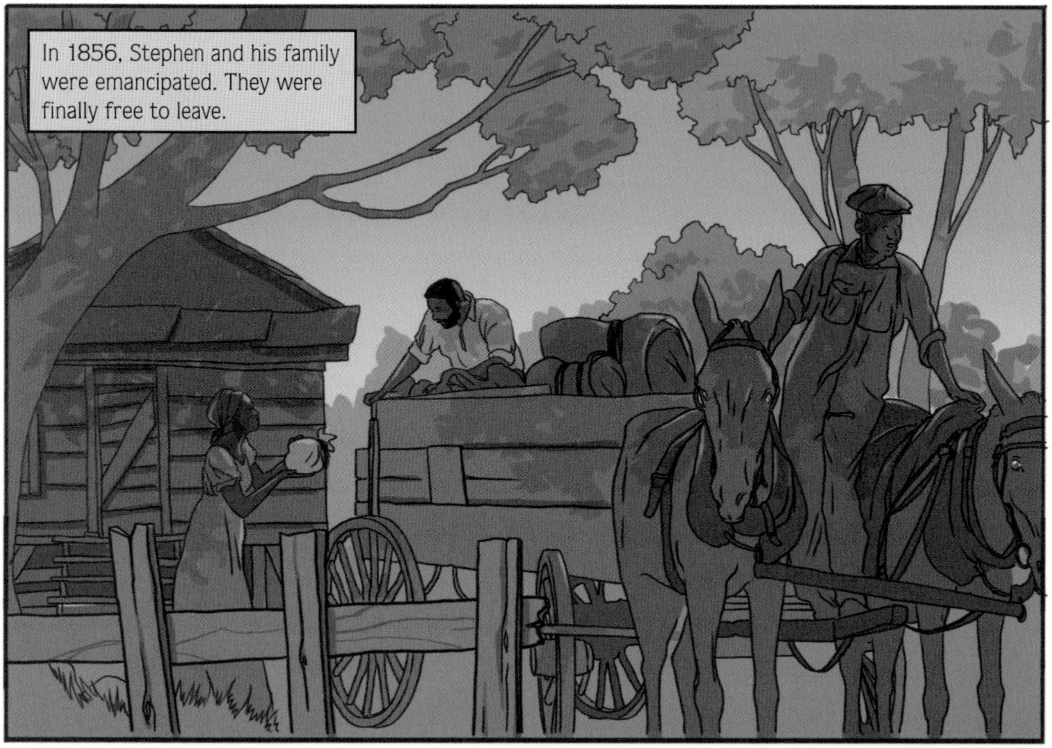
In 1856, Stephen and his family were emancipated. They were finally free to leave.

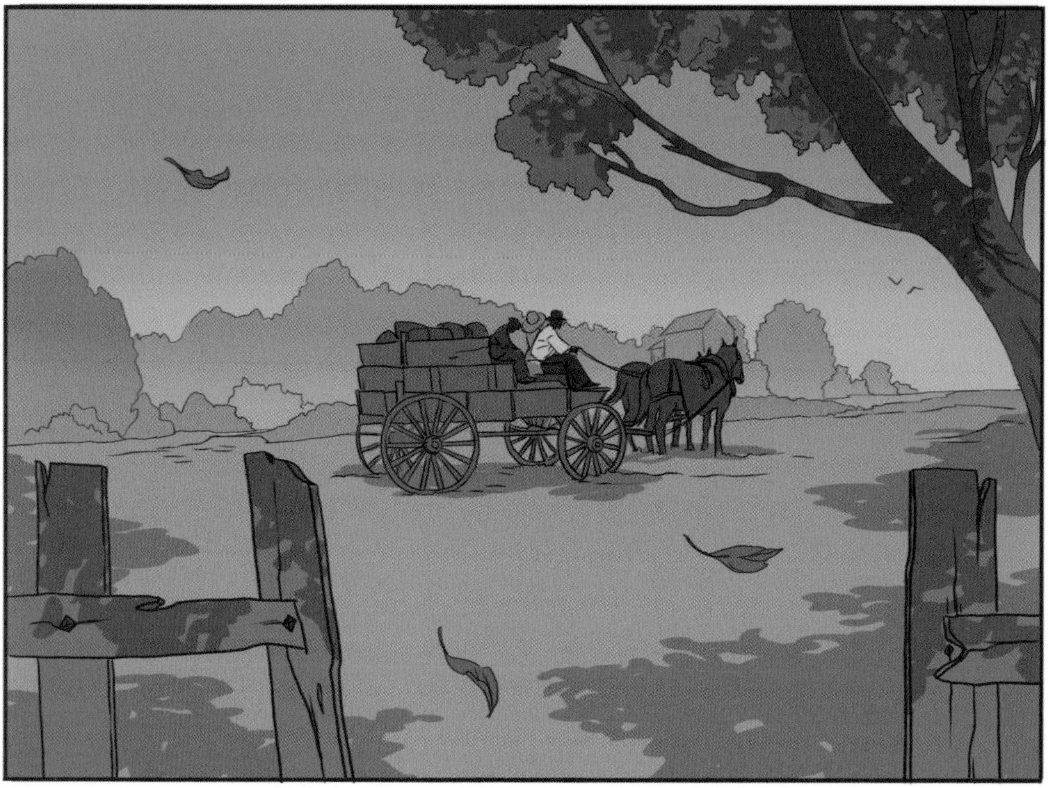

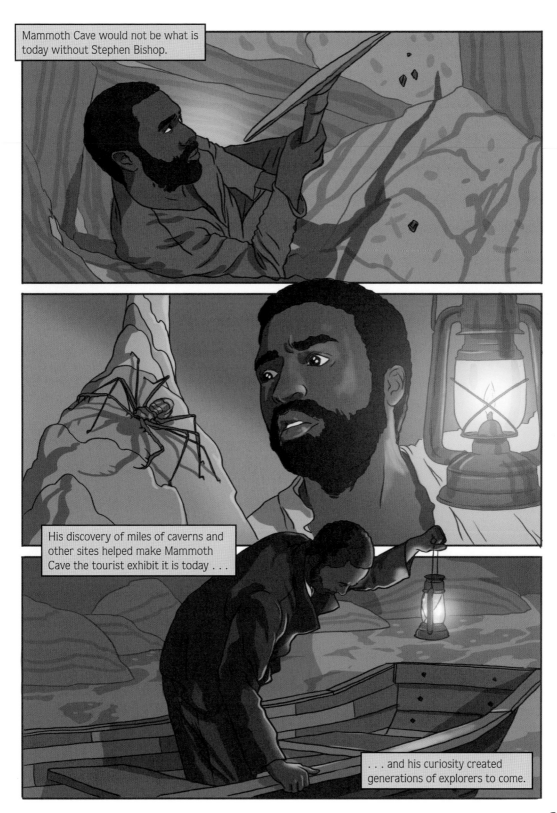

Mammoth Cave would not be what is today without Stephen Bishop.

His discovery of miles of caverns and other sites helped make Mammoth Cave the tourist exhibit it is today . . .

. . . and his curiosity created generations of explorers to come.

MORE ABOUT STEPHEN BISHOP AND MAMMOTH CAVES

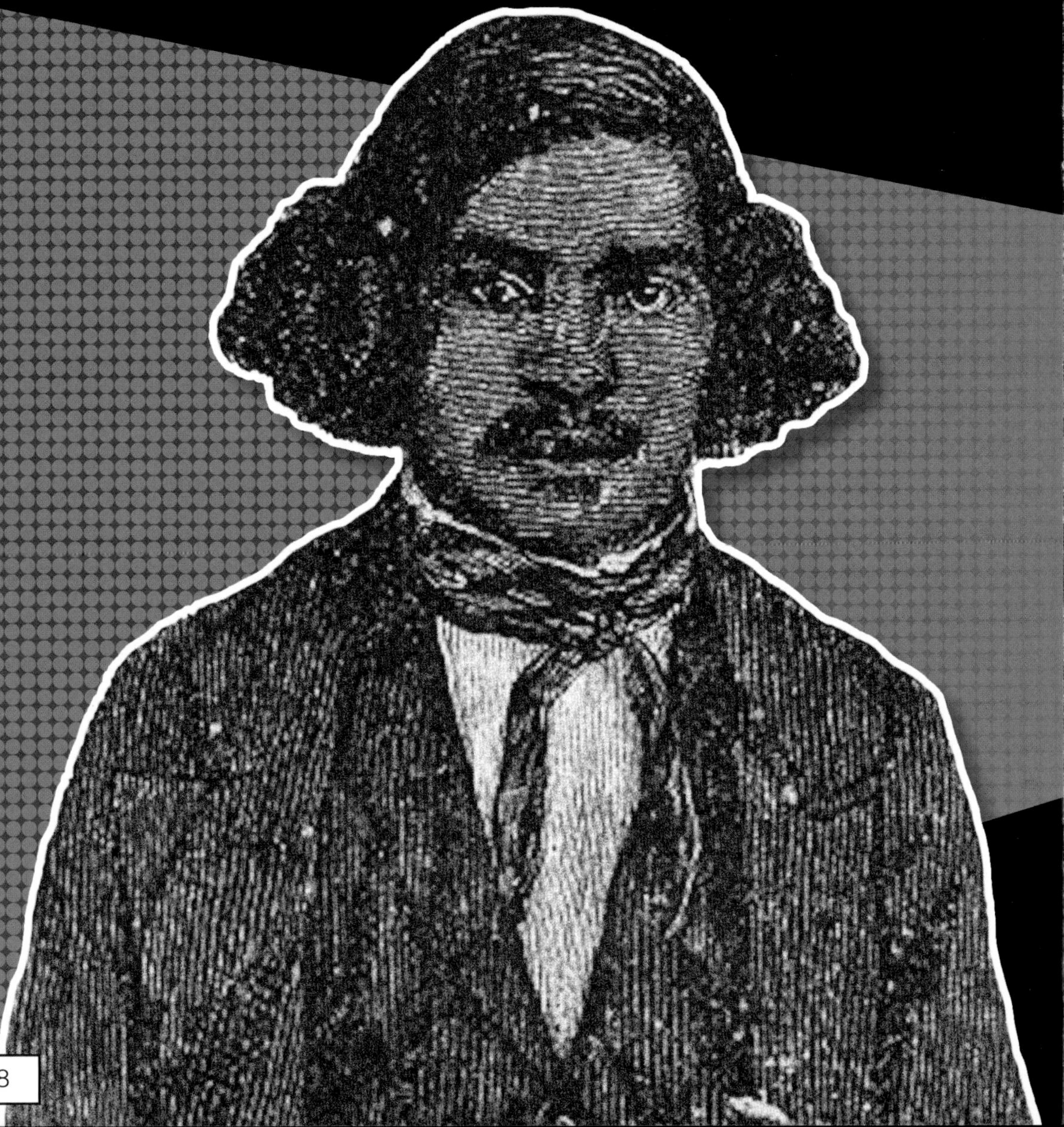

- Historians believe that Stephen Bishop learned to speak some Latin and Greek and to read and write by spending time with wealthy tourists. His personality and intelligence made the tourist feel comfortable and safe.

- The map that Stephen Bishop drew of Mammoth Cave for Dr. John Croghan was published in 1844.

- Even though tour guides like Stephen Bishop were always responsible for tourists' safety, they were never allowed to eat or be around them after the tour was done.

- If a tourist got hurt during a tour of the cave, it was up to Stephen to help or carry them out of the cave and to treat them, even if the person outweighed Stephen.

- Over 400 miles (643.7 km) of linking caves in the national park have been officially mapped.

- Mammoth Cave is the second largest tourist attraction in the United States. Niagara Falls is number one.

- Mammoth Cave is also the home of many endangered species such as Kentucky cave shrimp, the gray bat, and the Indiana bat.

GLOSSARY

cavern (KAV-ern)—cave or chamber

emancipated (ih-MAN-suh-pay-tid)—freed from enslavement

enslaved (en-SLAYVD)—forced to work for no pay and having no freedom or rights

geology (jee-OL-uh-jee)—a science that deals with the study of Earth

gypsum (JIP-suhm)—a type of mineral

miner (MYE-ner)—a person who works in a mine

minerals (MIN-er-uhls)—substances that are formed naturally in the earth

stalactite (stuh-LAK-tyte)—rock formations that look like icicles that grow down from the ceiling of a cave

tourist (TOOR-ist)—a person who is visiting a place

underground (UHN-der-GROUND)—beneath the surface of the ground

READ MORE

Beckerman, Neil Cross. *Caves*. New York: Orchard Books, 2022.

Henson, Heather. *Lift Your Light a Little Higher: The Story of Stephen Bishop*. New York: Atheneum Books for Young Readers, 2016.

Johnson, Catherine. *Race to the Frozen North: The Matthew Henson Story*. Edinburgh, Scotland: Barrington Stoke Ltd., 2018.

INTERNET SITES

Mammoth Cave
nps.gov/maca/index.htm

Stephen Bishop
nps.gov/people/stephen-bishop.htm

Stephen Bishop Facts for Kids
kids.kiddle.co/Stephen_Bishop_(cave_explorer)

ABOUT THE AUTHOR

Shawn Pryor is the creator and co-author of the graphic novel mystery series Cash and Carrie, co-creator and author of the 2019 GLYPH-nominated football/drama series Force, and author of *Kentucky Kaiju* and *Jake Maddox: Diamond Double Play*. In his free time, he enjoys reading, cooking, listening to streaming music playlists, and talking about why Zack from the *Mighty Morphin Power Rangers* is the greatest superhero of all time.

ABOUT THE ILLUSTRATOR

Alessandro Valdrighi studied at the prestigious Accademia di Belle Arti (Academy of Fine Arts) in Florence, Italy, and graduated with a bachelor's degree as a set designer. Alessandro learned to draw at an early age by copying comics and illustrations from books. He believes this is the reason he is now successful using multiple art styles. Alessandro lives and works in Siena, Italy, with his wife and two daughters, and a crazy cat.